A
STRAIGHTFORWARD GUIDE
TO
THE RIGHTS
OF
DISABLED PEOPLE

Doreen Jarrett

Straightforward Guides

ISBN 978-1-84716-899-3

Printed by 4Edge Ltd www.4Edge.co.uk

Editor: Roger Sproston

Cover design by Bookworks Derby

Contents

Introduction

****

Introduction

This is the Revised edition of *A Straightforward Guide to The Rights of Disabled people,* updated to **2019.** The book is aimed primarily at people with physical disabilities and is wide ranging, dealing with everything from benefits, employment travel, rights in the home and disabled servicemen and women.

Currently, at the time of writing, 2019, there are real ongoing fears that the benefits and security enjoyed by people with disabilities are under attack, mainly through the governments approach to reducing the overall welfare bill. It is feared that the introduction of benefits such as Personal Independence Payments, which replace Disability Living Allowance for those under 65 and also the abolition of the Independent Living Fund, will in the longer-term have an effect on disabled people and their incomes. This is because, in the main, disabled people find it harder to enter the workplace and sustain employment that others.

This book covers the benefit system in it's entirety and highlights what you may or may not be entitled to. It also covers carer's rights and the law governing those rights, the Care Act 2014. Form thereon we discuss employment law as it affects disabled people, education, care homes, rights whilst in hospital,, rights in the home, disabled children,, rights whilst travelling, rights for ex-service personnel and general rights covering the payment of income tax.

Finally, at the end of the book there are useful addresses and websites of organisations who deal with all areas of disability.
It should be noted that much of the information contained in the book relates to England and Wales. For information specific to Scotland visit www.disabilityscot.org.uk and Northern Ireland www.nidirect.gov.uk/.../your-rights-if-you-have-disability.

This book sets out to educate and inform those with physical disabilities, their carer's and also parents of disabled people, whether adult or child.

Chapter 1

The Law and Disability

The law and disability
In general, the wide body of laws that protect all people in the United Kingdom will apply to disabled people. Such laws can include consumer law, employment law and family law. However, in certain important respects, the law that applies to disabled people, and gives an extra layer of protection is the Equality Act 2010. This law is wide ranging and incorporated many previous Acts, such as the Disability Discrimination Act, and also clearly defines discrimination. Below is a summary of the Act. However, as we go through the book continuous reference will be made to the Act as it applies to the many areas of life, such as employment and transport, that directly affects disabled people.

The Equality Act 2010
The Equality Act 2010 prohibits discrimination against people with the protected characteristics that are specified in section 4 of the Act. Disability is one of the specified protected characteristics. Protection from discrimination for disabled people applies to disabled people in a range of circumstances, covering the provision of goods, facilities and services, the exercise of public functions, premises, work, education, and associations. Only those people who are defined as disabled in accordance with section 6 of the Act, and the associated Schedules and regulations made under that section, will be entitled to the protection that the Act provides to disabled people. However, importantly, the Act also provides protection for non-disabled people who are subjected to direct discrimination or harassment because of their association with a

disabled person or because they are wrongly perceived to be disabled.

The Act defines a disabled person as, simply, a person with a disability. A person has a disability for the purposes of the Act if he or she has a physical or mental impairment and the impairment has a substantial and long-term adverse effect on his or her ability to carry out normal day-to-day activities

This means that, in general:

- the person must have an impairment that is either physical or mental
- the impairment must have adverse effects which are substantial
- the substantial adverse effects must be long-term and
- the long-term substantial adverse effects must have an effect on normal day-to-day activities

Definition of 'impairment'

The definition requires that the effects which a person may experience must arise from a physical or mental impairment. The term mental or physical impairment should be given its ordinary meaning. It is not necessary for the cause of the impairment to be established, nor does the impairment have to be the result of an illness. In many cases, there will be no dispute as to whether a person has an impairment. Any disagreement is more likely to be about whether the effects of the impairment are sufficient to fall within the definition and in particular whether they are long-term. This is a crucial fact.

Whether a person is disabled for the purposes of the Act is generally determined by reference to the effect that an impairment has on that person's ability to carry out normal day-to-day activities. An exception to this is a person with severe disfigurement. A disability can arise from a wide range of impairments which can be:

- sensory impairments, such as those affecting sight or hearing;
- impairments with fluctuating or recurring effects such as Rheumatoid arthritis, Myalgic encephalitis (ME), Chronic fatigue syndrome (CFS), Fibromyalgia, Depression and Epilepsy;
- progressive, such as Motor neurone disease, Muscular dystrophy, and forms of Dementia;
- auto-immune conditions such as Systemic lupus erythematosis (SLE);
- organ specific, including Respiratory conditions, such as Asthma, and cardiovascular diseases, including Thrombosis, Stroke and Heart disease;
- developmental, such as Autistic spectrum disorders (ASD), Dyslexia and Dyspraxia;
- learning disabilities;
- mental health conditions with symptoms such as anxiety, low mood, panic attacks, phobias, or unshared perceptions; eating disorders; bipolar affective disorders; obsessive compulsive disorders; personality disorders; post traumatic stress disorder, and some self-harming behaviour;
- Mental illnesses, such as depression and schizophrenia;
- produced by injury to the body, including to the brain.

Persons with HIV infection, cancer and multiple sclerosis
The Act states that a person who has cancer, HIV infection or Multiple sclerosis (MS) is a disabled person. This means that the person is protected by the Act effectively from the point of diagnosis.

Certain conditions are not regarded as impairments. These are:

- o   addiction to, or dependency on, alcohol, nicotine, or any other substance (other than in consequence of the substance being medically prescribed);
- o   the condition known as seasonal allergic rhinitis (e.g. hayfever), except where it aggravates the effect of another condition;
- o   tendency to set fires;
- o   tendency to steal;
- o   tendency to physical or sexual abuse of other persons;
- o   exhibitionism;

A person with an excluded condition may nevertheless be protected as a disabled person if he or she has an accompanying impairment which meets the requirements of the definition. For example, a person who is addicted to a substance such as alcohol may also have depression, or a physical impairment such as liver damage, arising from the alcohol addiction. While this person would not meet the definition simply on the basis of having an addiction, he or she may still meet the definition as a result of the effects of the depression or the liver damage.

Disfigurements which consist of a tattoo (which has not been removed), non-medical body piercing, or something attached through such piercing, are treated as not having a substantial adverse effect on the person's ability to carry out normal day-to-day activities.

The Act says that, except for the provisions in Part 12 (Transport) and section 190 (improvements to let dwelling houses), the provisions of the Act also apply in relation to a person who previously has had a disability as defined in the Act. This means that someone who is no longer disabled, but who met the requirements of the definition in the past, will still be covered by the Act. Also protected would be someone who continues to experience debilitating effects as a result of treatment for a past disability.

Definition of 'long-term effects'

The Act states that, for the purpose of deciding whether a person is disabled, a long-term effect of an impairment is one:

- which has lasted at least 12 months; or
- where the total period for which it lasts, from the time of the first onset, is likely to be at least 12 months; or
- which is likely to last for the rest of the life of the person affected

Special provisions apply when determining whether the effects of an impairment that has fluctuating or recurring effects are long-term. Also a person who is deemed to be a disabled person does not need to satisfy the long-term requirement.

The cumulative effect of related impairments should be taken into account when determining whether the person has experienced a long-term effect for the purposes of meeting the definition of a disabled person. The substantial adverse effect of an impairment which has developed from, or is likely to develop from, another impairment should be taken into account when determining whether the effect has lasted, or is likely to last at least twelve months, or for the rest of the life of the person affected.

Normal day-to-day activities

In general, day-to-day activities are things people do on a regular or daily basis, and examples include shopping, reading and writing, having a conversation or using the telephone, watching television, getting washed and dressed, preparing and eating food, carrying out household tasks, walking and travelling by various forms of transport, and taking part in social activities. Normal day-to-day activities can include general work-related activities, and study and education-related activities, such as interacting with colleagues, following instructions, using a computer, driving, carrying out interviews, preparing written documents, and keeping to a timetable or a shift pattern.

The term 'normal day-to-day activities' is not intended to include activities which are normal only for a particular person, or a small group of people. In deciding whether an activity is a normal day-to-day activity, account should be taken of how far it is carried out by people on a daily or frequent basis. In this context, 'normal' should be given its ordinary, everyday meaning.

A normal day-to-day activity is not necessarily one that is carried out by a majority of people. For example, it is possible that some activities might be carried out only, or more predominantly, by people of a particular gender, such as breast-feeding or applying make-up, and cannot therefore be said to be normal for most people. They would nevertheless be considered to be normal day-to-day activities.

Also, whether an activity is a normal day-to-day activity should not be determined by whether it is more normal for it to be carried out at a particular time of day. For example, getting out of bed and getting dressed are activities that are normally associated with the morning. They may be carried out much later in the day by workers who work night shifts, but they would still be considered to be normal day-to-day activities. The following examples demonstrate a range of day-to-day effects on impairment:

- o Difficulty in getting dressed,
- o Difficulty carrying out activities associated with toileting, or caused by frequent minor incontinence;
- o Difficulty preparing a meal,
- o Difficulty eating;
- o Difficulty going out of doors unaccompanied, for example, because the person has a phobia, a physical restriction, or a learning disability;
- o Difficulty waiting or queuing,

16

- o Difficulty using transport; for example, because of physical restrictions, pain or fatigue, a frequent need for a lavatory or as a result of a mental impairment or learning disability;
- o Difficulty in going up or down steps, stairs or gradients;
- o A total inability to walk, or an ability to walk only a short distance without difficulty;
- o Difficulty entering or staying in environments that the person perceives as strange or frightening;
- o Behaviour which challenges people around the person, making it difficult for the person to be accepted in public places;
- o Persistent difficulty crossing a road safely,
- o Persistent general low motivation or loss of interest in everyday activities;
- o Difficulty accessing and moving around buildings;
- o Difficulty operating a computer, for example, because of physical restrictions in using a keyboard, a visual impairment or a learning disability;
- o Difficulty picking up and carrying objects of moderate weight, such as a bag of shopping or a small piece of luggage, with one hand;
- o Inability to converse, or give instructions orally, in the person's native spoken language;
- o Difficulty understanding or following simple verbal instructions;
- o Difficulty hearing and understanding another person speaking clearly over the voice telephone
- o Persistent and significant difficulty in reading or understanding written material where this is in the person's native written language,
- o Frequent confused behaviour, intrusive thoughts, feelings of being controlled, or delusions;

- o Persistently wanting to avoid people or significant difficulty taking part in normal social interaction or forming social relationships,
- o Persistent difficulty in recognising, or remembering the names of, familiar people such as family or friends;
- o Persistent distractibility or difficulty concentrating;
- o Compulsive activities or behaviour, or difficulty in adapting after a reasonable period to minor changes in a routine.

Whether a person satisfies the definition of a disabled person for the purposes of the Act will depend upon the full circumstances of the case. That is, whether the substantial adverse effect of the impairment on normal day-to-day activities is long term.

Specialised activities
Where activities are themselves highly specialised or involve highly specialised levels of attainment, they would not be regarded as normal day-to-day activities for most people. In some instances work-related activities are so highly specialised that they would not be regarded as normal day-to-day activities. The same is true of other specialised activities such as playing a musical instrument to a high standard of achievement; taking part in activities where very specific skills or level of ability are required; or playing a particular sport to a high level of ability, such as would be required for a professional footballer or athlete. Where activities involve highly specialised skills or levels of attainment, they would not be regarded as normal day-to-day activities for most people.

Normal day-to-day activities also include activities that are required to maintain personal well-being or to ensure personal safety, or the safety of other people. Account should be taken of whether the effects of an impairment have an impact on whether the person is inclined to carry out or neglect basic functions such as eating, drinking, sleeping, keeping warm or personal hygiene; or to exhibit behaviour which puts the person or other people at risk.

Indirect effects

An impairment may not directly prevent someone from carrying out one or more normal day-to-day activities, but it may still have a substantial adverse effect on how the person carries out those activities. For example pain or fatigue: where an impairment causes pain or fatigue, the person may have the ability to carry out a normal day-to-day activity, but may be restricted in the way that it is carried out because of experiencing pain in doing so. Or the impairment might make the activity more than usually fatiguing so that the person might not be able to repeat the task over a sustained period of time.

Disabled children

The effects of impairments may not be apparent in babies and young children because they are too young to have developed the ability to carry out activities that are normal for older children and adults. Regulations provide that an impairment to a child under six years old is to be treated as having a substantial and long-term adverse effect on the ability of that child to carry out normal day-to-day activities where it would normally have a substantial and long-term adverse effect on the ability of a person aged six years or over to carry out normal day-to-day activities.

Children aged six and older are subject to the normal requirements of the definition. That is, that they must have an impairment which has a substantial and long-term adverse effect on their ability to carry out normal day-to-day activities. However, in considering the ability of a child aged six or over to carry out a normal day-to-day activity, it is necessary to take account of the level of achievement which would be normal for a person of a similar age.

Part 6 of the Act provides protection for disabled pupils and students by preventing discrimination against them at school or in post-16 education because of, or for a reason related to, their disability. A pupil or student must satisfy the definition of disability as described in this guidance in order to be protected by Part 6 of the Act. The duties for schools in the Act, including the duty for schools to make reasonable adjustments for disabled children, are designed to dovetail with duties under the Special Educational Needs (SEN) framework which are based on a separate definition of special educational needs. Further information on these duties can be found in the SEN Code of Practice and the Equality and Human Rights Commission's Codes of Practice for Education.

****

Chapter 2

The Benefits System-What You Are Entitled To

As we have seen in Chapter 1, the Equality Act 2010 is central to every aspect of disability, and that includes benefits for disabled people.

Very often, disabled people are prevented from entering the workplace and earning a living, It follows that there will be a reliance on benefits to at least ensure a decent standard of living. In this chapter, we will be looking at the range of benefits available, including those benefits specifically aimed at disabled people and also benefits which are aimed at everyone. They cover everything which a disabled person might need to ensure that day to day living is taken care of. All rates quoted cover the year 2018-2019.

We will be looking at the following benefits:

- ➢ Attendance Allowance
- ➢ Personal Independence Payment
- ➢ Carers Allowance
- ➢ Housing Benefit
- ➢ Council Tax Support
- ➢ Pension Credit
- ➢ Income Support
- ➢ Job Seekers Allowance
- ➢ Employment and Support Allowance
- ➢ Universal Credit
- ➢ Tax Credits

- ➤ Winter Fuel payment
- ➤ Cold weather Payment
- ➤ TV Licence Concessions
- ➤ Bereavement Allowance

Attendance Allowance

You should be able to claim Attendance Allowance if your ability to look after your own personal care is affected by physical or mental illness or disability. Attendance Allowance has 2 weekly rates, and the rate you get very much depends on the help you need.

The current rates are:

- £57.30 if you need help in the day or at night
- £85.60 if you need help both in the day and at night.

Claiming Attendance Allowance won't affect any other income you receive, and it's also tax-free. If you are awarded it, you may become entitled to other benefits, such as Pension Credit, Housing Benefit or Council Tax Reduction, or an increase in these benefits.

You may be eligible for Attendance Allowance if you are 65 or over (if you're under 65, you may be eligible for Personal Independence Payment instead-see below), could benefit from help with personal care, such as getting washed or dressed, or supervision to keep you safe during the day or night, have any type of disability or illness, including sight or hearing impairments, or mental health issues such as dementia and have needed help for at least 6 months. (If you're terminally ill you can make a claim straight away.)

Attendance Allowance isn't means-tested, so your income and savings aren't taken into account. You don't actually have to receive help from a carer, as Attendance Allowance is based on the help you need, not the help you actually get. Also, you don't strictly have to spend your Attendance Allowance on care – it's up to you how you use it. You can get a claim form by calling the Attendance Allowance helpline on 0800 731 0122 or textphone: 0800 731 0317. You can also download a claim form or claim online.

Attendance Allowance doesn't usually take into account problems with housework, cooking, shopping and gardening. If your application is turned down, ask an advice agency such as Citizens Advice about whether you should challenge the decision. Many applications are turned down because people don't mention or aren't clear about how their illness or disability affects their lives.

If you are not a citizen of the uk you should check the eligibility rules. You can contact your nearest Citizens Advice for help.

If you're an EEA national living in the UK , you'll need to meet the habitual residence test. If you get a pension from an EEA country, you might not be entitled to Attendance Allowance - get advice before you claim. You normally can't apply if you're subject to immigration control, for example if you need a visa to live or work in the UK, or you have a visa that says "no recourse to public funds".

If you're terminally ill
If you're not expected to live for more than 6 months, there are 'special rules':

- there's no qualifying period for how long you've had your illness
- if you're eligible, you'll automatically get the higher rate of Attendance Allowance

If you're in a care home
You cannot usually get Attendance Allowance if you live in a care home and your care is paid for by your local authority. You can still claim Attendance Allowance if you pay for all your care home costs yourself.

Assessment

You might get a letter saying you need to attend an assessment to check your eligibility. The letter will explain why and where you must go. At the assessment, you'll be asked for identification. You can use a passport or any 3 of the following:

- birth certificate
- a full driving licence
- life assurance policy
- bank statements

You cannot get Attendance Allowance if you already get Disability Living Allowance (DLA) or Personal Independence Payment (PIP).

Personal Independence payment (PIP)

Personal Independence Payment (PIP) can help you with some of the extra costs if you have a long term ill-health or disability. The amount you get depends on how your condition affects you, not the condition itself. You'll be assessed by a health professional to work out the level of help you can get. Your rate will be regularly reviewed to make sure you're getting the right support.

If you get Disability Living Allowance

Disability Living Allowance (DLA) is ending for people aged 16 to 64. You can keep getting DLA if you're under 16 or you were born on or before 8 April 1948 and have an existing claim. You'll continue getting DLA until the Department for Work and Pensions (DWP) invites you to apply for PIP. You do not need to do anything until DWP writes to you about your DLA unless your circumstances change.

*

Eligibility

You must be aged 16 or over and have not reached State Pension age to claim.You must also have a health condition or disability where you:

- have had difficulties with daily living or getting around (or both) for 3 months
- expect these difficulties to continue for at least 9 months (unless you're terminally ill with less than 6 months to live)

You must have lived in England, Scotland or Wales for at least 2 of the last 3 years, and be in one of these countries when you apply. If you've recently returned from living in another EEA country, you might be able to get PIP sooner. You can get PIP whether you're working or not. You cannot get PIP and Armed Forces Independence Payment at the same time. There are additional rules if you live abroad or if you're not a British citizen.

Living abroad

You might still be able to get PIP if you:

- live in another EU or EEA country or Switzerland - you can only get help with daily living needs
- are a member or family member of the Armed Forces

If you're not a British citizen

You must:

- normally live in or show that you intend to settle in the UK, the Republic of Ireland, Isle of Man or the Channel Islands
- not be subject to immigration control (unless you're a sponsored immigrant)

You might still be able to get PIP if you are a refugee or have humanitarian protection status.

Daily living difficulties

You may get the daily living part of PIP if you need help more than half of the time with things like:

- preparing or eating food
- washing, bathing and using the toilet
- dressing and undressing
- reading and communicating
- managing your medicines or treatments
- making decisions about money
- engaging with other people

Mobility difficulties

You may get the Mobility part of PIP if you need help going out or moving around.

How you're assessed

You'll be assessed by an independent healthcare professional to help DWP work out the level of help you need.

What you'll get

Personal Independence Payment (PIP) is usually paid every 4 weeks. It's tax free and you can get it whether you're in or out of work. You'll need an assessment to work out the level of help you'll get. Your rate will be regularly reviewed to make sure you're getting the right support. PIP is made up of 2 parts. Whether you get one or both of these and how much you'll get depends on how severely your condition affects you.

Daily living part

The weekly rate for the daily living part of PIP is either £57.30 or £85.60.

Mobility part

The weekly rate for the mobility part of PIP is either £22.65 or £59.75.

Terminal illness

You'll get the higher daily living part if you're not expected to live more than 6 months. The rate of the mobility part depends on your needs.

How other benefits affect your PIP

If you get PIP and Constant Attendance Allowance, the 'daily living' part of your PIP will be reduced by the amount of Constant Attendance Allowance you get.

Other help

You or your carer might also qualify for other financial help, for example Carer's Allowance, or help with housing or transport costs. If you get PIP and you work, you might also be able to get the disability element of Working Tax Credit (up to £3,090 a year, or up to £4,420 if your disability is severe). You can contact HMRC to find out.

How to claim

You can make a new Personal Independence Payment (PIP) claim by calling the Department for Work and Pensions (DWP). Someone else can call on your behalf, but you'll need to be with them when they call. There are also other ways to claim if you find it difficult to use a telephone.

Claim by telephone or textphone

Before you call, you'll need:

- your contact details, for example telephone number
- your date of birth

- your National Insurance number - this is on letters about tax, pensions and benefits
- your bank or building society account number and sort code
- your doctor or health worker's name, address and telephone number
- dates and addresses for any time you've spent abroad, in a care home or hospital

DWP - PIP claims

Telephone: 0800 917 2222

Textphone: 0800 917 7777

NGT text relay (if you cannot hear or speak on the phone): 18001 then 0800 917 2222

Calling from abroad: +44 191 218 7766

Monday to Friday, 8am to 6pm

Claim by post

You can get a form to send information by post (although this can delay the decision on your claim). Write a letter to ask for the form.

Personal Independence Payment New Claims

Post Handling Site B

Wolverhampton

WV99 1AH

What happens next

- You'll be sent a 'How your disability affects you' form. Call the PIP enquiry line if you need it in an alternative format such as braille, large print or audio CD.
- Fill in the form using the notes that come with it to help you.
- Return the form to DWP - the address is on the form.

- To assess the level of help you need, an independent health professional will either invite you to a meeting or ask your health or social care worker for information.
- If you're invited to a meeting, you'll be asked questions about your ability to carry out activities and how your condition affects your daily life. The meeting can be either at your home or at an assessment centre, and will take about an hour.
- You'll get a letter that tells you whether you'll get PIP. If you do, you'll be told how much you'll get and the date it will be reviewed so that you continue to get the right support.

If you're terminally ill

You can get PIP more quickly if you're not expected to live more than 6 months.

Call DWP to start your PIP claim. Ask a doctor or other healthcare professional for form DS1500. They'll either fill it in and give the form to you or send it directly to DWP.

Video relay service if you're terminally ill

If you're deaf and use British Sign Language (BSL) you may be able to use the Video Relay Service.

If you disagree with a decision

You can challenge a decision about your claim. This is called asking for 'mandatory reconsideration'.

If your PIP claim is reviewed

The letter you got when your Personal Independence Payment (PIP) was approved will tell you when your claim will end and if it will be reviewed. If your claim is going to be reviewed, the letter will tell you when you'll be contacted about the review.

How PIP reviews work

1. You'll get a letter asking you to fill in a form called 'Award review - how your disability affects you'.
2. Fill in the form using the notes that come with it.
3. Send the form and any supporting information you have not shared with the Department for Work and Pensions (DWP) before - the form explains what to include and where to send it.
4. DWP will review your form. You might be asked to go to a face-to-face meeting with an independent health professional to discuss how your condition affects your daily life.
5. You'll get a letter that tells you what will happen with your PIP. If your needs have changed, your PIP might be increased, reduced or stopped.

If you disagree with a decision

You can challenge a decision about your claim. This is called asking for mandatory reconsideration.

Carer's Allowance

The main welfare benefit for carers is called Carer's Allowance and it's worth £64.60 per week if you're eligible. You don't have to be related to or live with the person you care for to claim Carer's Allowance. You'll also get National Insurance credits each week towards your pension if you're under pension age.

You may not think of yourself as a carer. Perhaps you've looked after someone for a long time without ever calling yourself one, or maybe you think the help you give your spouse or parent is simply what you should be doing. If so, you may have been missing out on the help that is available to you. To claim Carer's Allowance, you must:

- spend at least 35 hours a week caring for a disabled person - you don't have to live with them
- The person you care for must receive:
  1. Personal Independence Payment - daily living component
  2. Disability Living Allowance - the middle or highest care rate
  3. Attendance Allowance
  4. Constant Attendance Allowance at or above the normal maximum rate with an Industrial Injuries Disablement Benefit
  5. Constant Attendance Allowance at the basic (full day) rate with a War Disablement Pension
  6. Armed Forces Independence Payment
- not be in full-time education.

Your eligibility

You must earn no more than £120 a week after tax and expenses. Expenses can include:

- 50% of your pension contributions
- some of the costs of caring for your children or the disabled person while you're at work

All of the following must also apply:

- you're 16 or over
- you spend at least 35 hours a week caring for someone
- you've been in England, Scotland or Wales for at least 2 of the last 3 years (this does not apply if you're a refugee or have humanitarian protection status)
- you normally live in England, Scotland or Wales, or you live abroad as a member of the armed forces
- you're not in full-time education
- you're not studying for 21 hours a week or more
- you're not subject to immigration control

You might still be eligible if you're moving to or already living in another EEA country or Switzerland.

You might be eligible for Carer's Credit if you're not eligible for Carer's Allowance. Carer's Allowance may not be paid if you're receiving a State Pension or certain other benefits, but it's still worth claiming because you could get extra Pension Credit and/or Housing Benefit.

If you're claiming Universal Credit You may be able to get an extra amount because of your caring role without having to apply for Carer's Allowance. (see below for universal credit).

If you want to make a claim for carers allowance call the Carer's Allowance Unit on 0800 731 0279 textphone 0800 731 0317 to request a claim pack. Or you can visit GOV.UK to download a claim form or make a claim online.

Housing benefit
Eligibility
Housing Benefit (HB) can help you pay your rent if you're unemployed, on a low income or claiming benefits. HB being replaced by Universal Credit. You can only make a new claim for Housing Benefit if one of the following is true:

- you are getting the severe disability premium
- you got the severe disability premium within the last month and you're still eligible for it
- you have reached State Pension age
- you live in temporary accommodation
- you live in sheltered or supported housing with special facilities such as alarms or wardens

If not, you'll need to claim Universal Credit instead. Usually you will not get Housing Benefit if:

- your savings are over £16,000 - unless you get Guarantee Credit of Pension Credit

- you're paying a mortgage on your own home - you may be able to get Support for Mortgage Interest (SMI)
- you live in the home of a close relative
- you're already claiming Universal Credit (unless you're in temporary or supported housing)
- your partner is already claiming Housing Benefit
- you're a full-time student - unless you're disabled
- you're residing in the UK as a European Economic Area jobseeker
- you're an asylum seeker or sponsored to be in the UK
- you're subject to immigration control and your granted leave states that you cannot claim public funds

Changes to Housing Benefit eligibility from 15 May 2019

From 15 May 2019, if you're in a couple you'll only be eligible to start getting Housing Benefit if either:

- you and your partner have both reached State Pension age
- one of you has reached State Pension age and started claiming Housing Benefit or Pension Credit (for you as a couple) before 15 May 2019

If you're not already getting Housing Benefit on 14 May 2019, you can backdate your claim. You could still be eligible to get Housing Benefit. You can ask for your claim to be backdated to 14 May or before. You'll need to apply by 13 August 2019 to do this. You can apply for Universal Credit instead if you're still not eligible.

If you already get Housing Benefit and you're in a couple

You'll continue to get Housing Benefit after 15 May 2019. If your entitlement stops for any reason, for example your circumstances change, you cannot start getting it again until you (or your partner) are eligible under the new rules.

If you already get Housing Benefit and you're single

From 15 May 2019, you'll stop getting Housing Benefit if you start living with a partner who is under State Pension age. You can start getting it again when your partner reaches State Pension age.

What you'll get

You may get help with all or part of your rent. There's no set amount of Housing Benefit and what you get will depend on whether you rent privately or from a council.

Use a benefits calculator to work out what you could get or check what extra help is available.

Council and social housing rent

How much you get depends on:

- your 'eligible' rent
- if you have a spare room
- your household income - including benefits, pensions and savings (over £6,000)
- your circumstances, for example the age of people in the house or if someone has a disability

Eligible rent

Eligible rent means the reasonable rent for a suitable property in your area. It includes service charges (such as for lift maintenance or a communal laundry) but not things like heating.

Spare bedrooms

Your Housing Benefit could be reduced if you live in council or social housing and have a spare bedroom. The reduction is:

- 14% of the 'eligible rent' for 1 spare bedroom
- 25% of the 'eligible rent' for 2 or more spare bedrooms

Example reduced Housing Benefit

Your eligible rent is £100 per week. Housing Benefit pays £50 and you pay £50. You have 1 spare bedroom so the reduction is 14%. This means your Housing Benefit will be reduced by £14 per week.

Sharing bedrooms

The following are expected to share:

- an adult couple
- 2 children under 16 of the same sex
- 2 children under 10 (regardless of sex)

The following can have their own bedroom:

- a single adult (16 or over)
- a child that would normally share but shared bedrooms are already taken, for example you have 3 children and 2 already share
- a couple or children who cannot share because of a disability or medical condition
- an overnight carer for you, your partner, your child or another adult - this is only if the carer does not live with you but sometimes has to stay overnight

One spare bedroom is allowed for:

- an approved foster carer who is between placements but only for up to 52 weeks from the end of the last placement
- a newly approved foster carer for up to 52 weeks from the date of approval if no child is placed with them during that time

Rooms used by students and members of the armed or reserve forces will not be counted as 'spare' if they're away and intend to return home.

Private rent

Local Housing Allowance (LHA) is used to work out Housing Benefit for tenants who rent privately. How much you get is usually based on:

- where you live
- your household size your income - including benefits, pensions and savings (over £6,000)
- your circumstances

How much you can get

Property	Weekly amount
1 bedroom (or shared accommodation)	Up to £268.46
2 bedrooms	Up to £311.40
3 bedrooms	Up to £365.09
4 bedrooms	Up to £429.53

Contact your local council if you're living in:

- a houseboat or a mooring
- a caravan site
- a room with any meals included in the rent (sometimes known as a boarding home)
- a hostel
- a Rent Act protected property

Exception

If you've been getting Housing Benefit since before 7 April 2008, these limits only apply if you:

- change address
- have a break in your claim for Housing Benefit

How you're paid

Housing Benefit is paid by your council as follows:

- council tenants - into your rent account (you will not receive the money)
- private tenants - into your bank or building society account (rarely by cheque)

The benefit cap

The benefit cap limits the total amount of benefit you can get. It applies to most people aged 16 or over who have not reached State Pension age. If you're affected, your Housing Benefit will go down to make sure that the total amount of benefit you get is not more than the cap level.

Appeal a Housing Benefit decision

Contact your local council to appeal a Housing Benefit decision.

How to claim

Housing Benefit is being replaced by Universal Credit. Most people will need to claim Universal Credit instead. Check you're eligible for Housing Benefit before you apply. How you claim Housing Benefit depends on whether you're also making a new claim for any other benefits. You'll need to provide evidence to support your claim.

If you're only applying for Housing Benefit

Apply through your local council if you're only making a new claim for Housing Benefit. You can still make a new claim if you're already getting other benefits.

If you're applying for other benefits

You can claim Housing Benefit as part of your application for other benefits. How you apply for Housing Benefit depends on which benefit you're applying for.

Employment and Support Allowance, Income Support or Jobseeker's Allowance

Contact Jobcentre Plus to claim Housing Benefit along with your application for the following benefits:

- Employment and Support Allowance
- Income Support
- Jobseeker's Allowance

Jobcentre Plus will send details of your claim for Housing Benefit to your council.

Jobcentre Plus

Telephone: 0800 055 6688

Textphone: 0800 023 4888

Pension Credit

Contact the Pension Service to claim Housing Benefit along with your application for Pension Credit. The Pension Service will send details of your claims for Housing Benefit to your council.

Pension Service

Telephone: 0800 99 1234

Textphone: 0800 169 0133

Universal Credit

You usually cannot get Universal Credit and Housing Benefit at the same time (unless you're in certain kinds of supported or temporary housing). You can get help paying for housing with your Universal Credit payment instead. You'll have to pay rent to your landlord directly.

Claiming in advance and backdating

You can claim in advance by up to 13 weeks (or 17 weeks if you're aged 60 or over), for example if you're moving. You will not usually get any money before you move. You might also be able to get your claim backdated - ask your council.

Appeal a decision

You can ask your council for a Housing Benefit decision to be reconsidered. If you're unhappy with the response you can appeal the decision.

Extra help to pay the rent

You could also apply for extra help from your council if your Housing Benefit does not cover your rent. This is called a Discretionary Housing Payment.

Universal Credit

If you're of working age and making a new claim in an area where Universal Credit has been introduced, you should claim Universal Credit to help with your rent. See below for more about Universal Credit.

Pension Credit

Pension Credit is an income-related benefit that comes in two parts and you may be eligible for one or both:

- Guarantee Credit tops up your weekly income to a guaranteed minimum level
- Savings Credit is extra money if you've got some savings or your income is higher than the basic State Pension

About 4 million older people are entitled to Pension Credit, yet about 1 in 3 of those eligible are still not claiming it. Don't be put off if you discover you're only eligible for a small amount of Pension Credit. It's your passport to other benefits, such as Housing Benefit and Council Tax Reduction. You may not be eligible for Savings Credit if you reached State Pension age on or after 6 April 2016.

Rates of Pension Credit

Guarantee Credit will top up your weekly income to:

- £163 if you're single
- or £248.80 if you're a couple.

If you qualify for Savings Credit, you can get up to:

- £13.40 extra per week if you're single
- or £14.99 if you're a couple.

Eligibility

To qualify for Pension Credit:

- you must live in England, Scotland or Wales
- you or your partner must have reached Pension Credit qualifying age

Your partner is your husband, wife or civil partner (if you live with them) or someone else you live with as if you were married.

You can read about Pension Credit in Northern Ireland.

Changes to Pension Credit eligibility from 15 May 2019

From 15 May 2019, if you're in a couple you'll only be eligible to start getting pension credit if either:

- you and your partner have both reached Pension Credit qualifying age
- one of you has reached Pension Credit qualifying age and is claiming Housing Benefit (for you as a couple)

If you're not already getting Pension Credit on 14 May 2019, you can backdate your claim. You could still be eligible to get Pension Credit. You can ask for your claim to be backdated to 14 May or before. You'll need to apply by 13 August 2019 to do this. You can apply for Universal Credit instead if you're still not eligible.

If you already get Pension Credit and you're in a couple
You'll continue to get Pension Credit after 15 May 2019. If your entitlement stops for any reason, for example your circumstances change, you cannot start getting it again until you (or your partner) are eligible under the new rules.

If you already get Pension Credit and you're single
From 15 May 2019, you'll stop getting Pension Credit if you start living with a partner who is under Pension Credit qualifying age. You can start getting it again when your partner reaches Pension Credit qualifying age.

Savings Credit
You can only start getting Savings Credit if you (and your partner, if you have one) reached State Pension age before 6 April 2016. If your partner did not reach State Pension age before 6 April 2016. If you've been getting Savings Credit since before 6 April 2016, you'll continue to get it as long as there are no breaks in your entitlement. If you stop being eligible for Savings Credit for any reason, you will not be able to get it again.

Working out your income
When you apply for Pension Credit your income is worked out. This includes:
- State Pension
- other pensions
- most social security benefits, for example Carer's Allowance
- savings, investments over £10,000 - for these £1 is counted for every £500 or part £500
- earnings

If you're entitled to a private or workplace pension, the amount you'd expect to get is calculated as income from the date you were able to get it, if you had claimed it. You will not get the benefit of deferring your State Pension if you or your partner are on Pension Credit, for example you will not build up extra State Pension or a lump sum for deferring your State Pension. When working out if you can get Pension Credit, the income you'd get from your State Pension is included whether you're claiming it or not. The calculation does not include:

- Attendance Allowance
- Christmas Bonus
- Disability Living Allowance
- Personal Independence Payment
- Housing Benefit
- Council Tax Reduction

If you're registered for Self Assessment, you must tell the Pension Service how much Income Tax you expect to pay for the current tax year - this affects how much Pension Credit you'll get.

Pension Credit if you leave Great Britain
Your entitlement to Pension Credit may be affected if you leave Great Britain (England, Scotland and Wales) for any period of time. You cannot get Pension Credit if you leave Great Britain permanently.

Pension Service helpline
Telephone: 0800 731 0469
Textphone: 0800 169 0133

Income Support
Income Support can help you cover your costs if you're on a low income.

You can only apply for Income Support if you either:

- get the severe disability premium
- got the severe disability premium in the last month, and are still eligible for it

If you cannot apply for Income Support you can apply for Universal Credit instead. All of the following must also apply to you (and your partner if you have one):

- you have no income or a low income, and no more than £16,000 in savings
- you're not in full-time paid work (you can work less than 16 hours a week, and your partner can work less than 24 hours a week)
- you're not eligible for Jobseeker's Allowance or Employment and Support Allowance
- you live in England, Scotland or Wales - there are different rules for Northern Ireland

You must also be between 16 and Pension Credit qualifying age, and at least one of the following:

- pregnant
- a lone parent (including a lone adoptive parent) with a child under 5
- a lone foster parent with a child under 16
- a single person looking after a child under 16 before they're adopted
- a carer
- on maternity, paternity or parental leave
- unable to work and you receive Statutory Sick Pay, Incapacity Benefit or Severe Disablement Allowance
- in full-time education (not university), aged between 16 and 20, and a parent

- in full-time education (not university), aged between 16 and 20, and not living with a parent or someone acting as a parent
- a refugee learning English - your course needs to be at least 15 hours a week, and you must have started it within 12 months of entering the UK
- in custody or due to attend court or a tribunal

You do not need a permanent address - for example, you can still claim if you:
- sleep rough
- live in a hostel or care home

What you'll get
You get:
- a basic payment (personal allowance)
- extra payments (premiums)

Your income and any savings (over £5,999) can affect how much you get.

Personal allowance
You must be at least 16 to get Income Support.

See overleaf.

Status	Age	Weekly payment
Single	16 to 24	£57.90

Status	Age	Weekly payment
Single	25 or over	£73.10
Lone parent	16 to 17	£57.90
Lone parent	18 or over	£73.10
Couples	Both under 18	£57.90
Couples	Both under 18 - 'higher rate'	£87.50
Couples	One under 18, the other 18 to 24	£57.90
Couples	One under 18, the other 25 or over	£73.10
Couples	One under 18, one over - 'higher rate'	£114.85
Couples	Both 18 or over	£114.85

Higher rate

You could get the higher rate if either of you is responsible for a child, or if each of you would be eligible for one of the following if you were not a couple:

- Employment and Support Allowance
- Income Support
- Jobseeker's Allowance

Premiums

You could also get an Income Support 'premium' - this is extra money based on your circumstances, for example if:

- your partner is a pensioner
- you're disabled or a carer

The benefit cap

The benefit cap limits the total amount of benefit you can get. It applies to most people aged 16 or over who have not reached State Pension age. Some individual benefits are not affected, but it may affect the total amount of benefit you get.

How you're paid

Payments are usually made every 2 weeks.

All benefits, pensions and allowances are paid into your bank, building society or credit union account. The quickest way to apply for Income Support is by phone.

New benefit claims
Jobcentre Plus - new claims

Telephone: 0800 169 0350

Textphone: 0800 023 4888

You can also apply by post by sending a claim form to your local Jobcentre Plus.

Jobseeker's Allowance

There are 3 different types of Jobseeker's Allowance (JSA):

- 'new style' JSA
- contribution-based JSA
- income-based JSA

Which types you can get depends on your circumstances. You can only apply for contribution-based and income-based JSA if you either:

- get the severe disability premium
- got the severe disability premium within the last month and are still eligible for it

If not, you can only apply for 'new style' JSA.

'New style' JSA

To be eligible for 'new style' JSA you'll need to have worked as an employee and paid Class 1 National Insurance contributions, usually in the last 2 to 3 years. National Insurance credits can also count. You will not be eligible if you were self-employed and only paid Class 2 National Insurance contributions, unless you were working as a share fisherman or a volunteer development worker. You'll also need to:

- be 18 or over
- be under the State Pension age
- not be in full-time education
- be available to work
- not be working at the moment, or be working less than 16 hours per week on average
- not have an illness or disability which stops you from working
- live in England, Scotland or Wales
- have the right to work in the UK

You'll also need to show you're looking for work to keep getting payments. our partner's income and savings will not affect your claim. ou can get 'new style' JSA for up to 182 days (about 6 months). After this you can talk to your work coach about your options.

Contribution-based JSA

You can only apply for contribution-based JSA if you either:
- get the severe disability premium
- got the severe disability premium within the last month and you're still eligible for it

To be eligible you will also need to have worked as an employee and paid Class 1 National Insurance contributions, usually in the last 2 to 3 years. National Insurance credits can also count. You will not be eligible if you were self-employed and only paid Class 2 National Insurance contributions, unless you were working as a share fisherman or a volunteer development worker.

You'll also need to:
- be 18 or over
- be under the State Pension age
- not be in full-time education
- be available to work
- not be working at the moment, or be working less than 16 hours per week on average
- not have an illness or disability which stops you from working
- live in England, Scotland or Wales
- have the right to work in the UK

You'll also need to show you're looking for work to keep getting payments. Your partner's income and savings will not affect your claim. You can get contribution-based JSA for up to 182 days (about 6 months). After this you can talk to your work coach about your options.

Income-based JSA

Your employment in the last 2 to 3 years does not affect your eligibility. You can only apply if you either:

- get the severe disability premium
- got the severe disability premium within the last month and you're still eligible for it
- You'll also need to:
- be 18 or over (there are some exceptions if you're 16 or 17 - contact Jobcentre Plus for advice)
- be under the State Pension age
- not be in full-time education
- be in England, Scotland or Wales
- be available for work
- not be working or be working on average less than 16 hours per week
- not have an illness or disability which stops you from working
- be single, or have a partner who works for less than 24 hours a week on average
- have £16,000 or less in savings (including your partner's savings)

How to claim or reclaim

You can usually apply for Jobseeker's Allowance (JSA) online. You cannot apply online if you get the severe disability premium, or got it in the last month and are still eligible for it. If you cannot apply online, call Jobcentre Plus.

Jobcentre Plus

Telephone: 0800 055 6688
Textphone: 0800 023 4888

After you make your claim

You'll get a text or phone call within 2 working days to arrange a JSA interview at your local Jobcentre Plus office.

Claim with your partner (joint claim)

You must make a joint claim if:

- neither you or your partner are responsible for a child
- you're applying for income-based JSA

If you disagree with a decision

You can challenge a decision about your claim. This is called asking for mandatory reconsideration. You'll also need to show you're looking for work.

Your JSA interview

Jobcentre Plus will contact you to arrange your interview after you've applied. At your JSA interview, you must sign an agreement about what steps you'll take to look for a job. This is called a 'Claimant Commitment'. You and your work coach will agree what goes in your Claimant Commitment.

Employment and Support Allowance

If you're ill or disabled, Employment and Support Allowance (ESA) offers you:

- financial support if you're unable to work
- personalised help so that you can work if you're able to

You can apply for ESA if you're employed, self-employed or unemployed. You might be transferred to ESA if you've been claiming other benefits like Income Support or Incapacity Benefit.

Work Capability Assessment

If you claim ESA you must have a Work Capability Assessment. This is to see to what extent your illness or disability affects your ability to work. You'll then be placed in one of 2 groups if you're entitled to ESA:

- work-related activity group, where you'll have regular interviews with an adviser
- support group, where you do not have interviews

What you'll get

How much ESA you get depends on:
- your circumstances, such as income
- the type of ESA you qualify for
- where you are in the assessment process

You can get financial support and work-related support through Employment and Support Allowance (ESA).

Financial support

You'll normally get the assessment rate for 13 weeks after your claim. This will be:
- up to £57.90 a week if you're aged under 25
- up to £73.10 a week if you're aged 25 or over

After that, if you're entitled to ESA, you'll be placed in one of 2 groups and will receive:
- up to £73.10 a week if you're in the work-related activity group
- up to £110.75 a week if you're in the support group

You might get more ESA in the work-related activity group if you applied before 3 April 2017. If you're in the support group and on income-related ESA, you're also entitled to the enhanced disability premium at £16.40 or £23.55 a week. You may also qualify for the severe disability premium at £64.30 or £128.60 a week. If the assessment takes longer than 13 weeks your benefit will be backdated to the 14th week of the claim.

The benefit cap

The benefit cap limits the total amount of benefit you can get. It applies to most people aged 16 or over who have not reached State Pension age. Some individual benefits are not affected, but it may affect the total amount of benefit you get. The cap will not affect you if you're in the support group.

Work-related support

Following your Work Capability Assessment you'll be placed in either the work-related activity group or support group if you're entitled to ESA.

Work-related activity group

You must go to regular interviews with an adviser who can help with things like job goals and improving your skills.

Support group

You do not have to go to interviews, but you can ask to talk to a personal adviser. You're usually in this group if your illness or disability severely limits what you can do.

How long you'll get ESA for

'New style' and contribution-based ESA last for 365 days if you're in the work-related activity group. There's no time limit if you're in the support group, or if you're getting income-based ESA.

Benefits sanctions

Your ESA can be reduced if you do not go to interviews or do work-related activity as agreed with your adviser. This reduction can continue for up to 4 weeks after you restart the interviews or activity. You'll get a 'sanction letter'. Tell your ESA adviser if you have a good reason for missing the interview. You'll get another letter if the decision is made to give you a sanction. Your benefit will only be affected once a decision has been made. You should contact your local council immediately if you claim Housing Benefit or Council Tax Reduction. They'll tell you what to do to continue getting support. If you get a sanction you can:

- ask for the decision to be looked at again
- ask for a 'hardship payment'

You will not get a sanction if you're in the support group.

Hardship payments

You may be able to get a hardship payment if your income-related ESA has been reduced because of a sanction or fraud penalty. You do not have to pay it back. A hardship payment is a reduced amount of your ESA (usually 60% or 80% of the basic rate, depending on your circumstances).

Eligibility

You can get a hardship payment if you cannot pay for rent, heating, food or other basic needs for you or your family. You must be 18 or over.

How to claim

Speak to your Jobcentre Plus adviser or work coach to find out how to claim a hardship payment.

Types of ESA

There are 3 different types of Employment and Support Allowance (ESA):

- 'new style' ESA
- contribution-based ESA
- income-based ESA

The type you get depends on your circumstances.

'New style' ESA

To get 'new style' ESA you'll need to have been an employee or self-employed and paid National Insurance contributions, usually in the last 2 to 3 years. National Insurance credits can also count. You'll also need to have an illness or disability that affects your ability to work. Your (or your partner's) income and savings will not affect how much 'new style' ESA you're paid.

'New style' ESA and Universal Credit

If you get both Universal Credit and 'new style' ESA at the same time, your 'new style' ESA payment will be deducted from your Universal Credit payment - you are not guaranteed to get any extra money.

Contribution-based ESA

You can only apply for contribution-based ESA if you have an illness or disability that affects your ability to work, and you either:
- get the severe disability premium
- got the severe disability premium within the last month and you're still eligible for it

You'll also need to have been an employee or self-employed and paid National Insurance contributions, usually in the last 2 to 3 years. National Insurance credits can also count. Your (or your partner's) income and savings will not affect how much contribution-based ESA you're paid.

Income-based ESA

You can only apply for income-based ESA if you have an illness or disability that affects your ability to work, and you either:
- get the severe disability premium
- got the severe disability premium within the last month and you're still eligible for it

Your National Insurance contributions in the last 2 to 3 years don't affect your eligibility.

Reapplying for ESA

You may be able to re-apply at least 12 weeks after your 'new style' or contribution-based ESA ends. You may qualify again depending on:

- what National Insurance contributions you paid in the last 2 full tax years before the tax year you're claiming in
- whether your health deteriorates and you're placed in the support group

You may get ESA if your illness or disability affects your ability to work and you're:

- under State Pension age
- not getting Statutory Sick Pay or Statutory Maternity Pay and you have not gone back to work
- not getting Jobseeker's Allowance

You can apply for ESA if you're:

- employed
- self-employed
- unemployed
- a student

If you've lived or worked abroad

You may be able to get ESA if you've paid enough UK National Insurance (or the equivalent in an EEA or other country with which the UK has an agreement).

Health and work conversation

You'll usually need to have a health and work conversation to discuss the support you need. You'll be told if you need one after you claim. If you do, it will take place around 4 weeks after the date of your claim. You might not need one, for example if you're in hospital or you have a terminal illness.

Work Capability Assessment

After you make a claim for ESA you'll get a letter telling you where to go for your Work Capability Assessment and explaining what to do. You must also fill in the 'Capability for work questionnaire' during the application. The questionnaire is different in Northern Ireland. You may be able to get a recording of the assessment.

Repeat claims

In most cases, you will not be eligible for ESA again if you were found capable of doing some work after your Work Capability Assessment. The main exceptions are where:

- your current condition has got a lot worse
- you're claiming for a new condition

Claiming ESA if you work

You might be able to work and still claim ESA. It depends on how much you'll get paid and the hours you do.

Permitted work

If you do 'permitted work' it will not usually affect your ESA. It's permitted work if both the following apply:

- you earn up to £125.50 a week
- you work less than 16 hours a week

There's no limit on how many weeks your permitted work can last for.

Supported permitted work

You can do 'supported permitted work' and earn up to £125.50 a week. Supported permitted work must be one of the following:

- part of a treatment programme
- supervised by someone from a local council or voluntary organisation whose job it is to arrange work for disabled people

When you start working

Fill in form PW1 and send it to the Jobcentre Plus office that deals with your benefit.

You need to tell Jobcentre Plus if you do any volunteer work (this normally does not affect your ESA).

Your income and savings

Your income may affect your income-related or contributory ESA. Income can include:

- you and your partner's income
- savings over £6,000
- pension income

You will not qualify for income-related ESA if you have savings over £16,000. 'New style' and contribution-based ESA do not take into account any savings you have.

How to claim

The quickest way to apply for Employment and Support Allowance (ESA) is by phone. The number you call depends on which type of ESA you're applying for. After you phone, you'll need to send your fit note (sometimes called 'sick note' or 'doctor's note').

You can only apply for contribution-based and income-based ESA if you either:

- get the severe disability premium

- got the severe disability premium within the last month and you're still eligible for it

If not, you can only apply for 'new style' ESA.

'New style' ESA
Apply for 'new style' ESA over the phone.
Telephone: 0800 328 5644
Textphone: 0800 328 1344

Contribution-based and income-related ESA
Call the contact centre to apply for contribution-based and income-related ESA.
Contact centre
Telephone: 0800 169 0350
Textphone: 0800 023 4888

You can also fill in and print out the ESA1 form and send or take it to your local Jobcentre Plus office. Call the contact centre to ask for accessible formats of the ESA1 form, such as braille, large print or audio CD.

Moving from incapacity benefits to ESA
You'll be told whether you're in the support group or work-related activity group if you're transferred from:
- Incapacity Benefit
- Income Support paid because of illness or disability
- Severe Disablement Allowance

You'll have a Work Capability Assessment to determine your ESA eligibility. If you're eligible, your benefit will be transferred automatically and there will not be a break in the payments you receive. If the amount of benefit you currently get is lower than the amount of ESA, your money will increase as soon as you move to ESA. You'll get a 'top-up payment' if the amount of benefit you currently get is more than the normal ESA amount. This means that you'll continue to get the same amount of money as you get now. The amount of benefit you get will not then rise until the normal amount of ESA has increased by the amount of the top-up payment.

Universal Credit

Universal Credit is a new benefit gradually being introduced nationally. It will eventually replace existing benefits:

- Income-based Jobseeker's Allowance
- Income-related Employment and Support Allowance
- Income Support
- Working Tax Credit
- Child Tax Credit
- Housing Benefit.

Who can get Universal Credit?

Universal Credit is gradually being rolled out across the UK, and it may not yet be available in the area where you live. To find out when Universal Credit will be rolled out in your area, contact Jobcentre Plus. You may be able to claim Universal Credit if you're out of work or on a low income. If you qualify for other benefits such as contribution-based Jobseeker's Allowance or contribution-based Employment and Support Allowance, you should claim them as well as Universal Credit.

The amount of Universal Credit you get will depend on a number of factors, such as the amount of hours you work or how much savings you have. You can't get Universal Credit if you have savings of more than £16,000. Standard Universal Credit payments per month are:

Single and under 25 £251.77
Single 25 and over £317.82
In a couple under 25 £395.20 (for both)
In a couple and 25 or over £498.89 (for both

You may be entitled to extra amounts if you have housing costs, caring responsibilities, dependent children

Extra amounts
You may get more money on top of your standard allowance if you're eligible.

If you have children
If you have 1 or 2 children, you'll get an extra amount for each child. If you have 3 or more children, you'll get an extra amount for at least 2 children. You can only get an extra amount for more children if any of the following are true:

- your children were born before 6 April 2017
- you were already claiming for 3 or more children before 6 April 2017
- other exceptions apply

You'll get an extra amount for any disabled or severely disabled child - no matter how many children you have or when they were born.

How much you will get	Extra monthly payment
For your first child	£277.08 (born before 6th April 2017
For your second child and (any other eligible children)	£231.67 per child
If you have a disabled or severely disabled child	£126.11 or £383.86
If you need help with childcare	

costs   Up to 85% of your costs (up to £646.35 for one child and £1108.04 for two or more children.

You might get the extra amount if you start caring for another child, depending on when they were born and how many children you have.

If you have a disability or health condition

How much you will get	Extra monthly amount
If you have limited capability for work and work related activity	£328.32

If you have limited capability for work and you started your health related universal credit or employment and support allowance claim before 3rd April 2017   £126.11

If you care for a severely disabled person

How much you will get	Extra monthly amount
If you provide care for at least 35 hours per week for a severely disabled person who receives a disability related benefit	£156.45

This is on top of any extra amount you get if you have a disabled child.

Housing costs

You could get money to help pay your housing costs. How much you get depends on your age and circumstances. The payment can cover rent and some service charges. If you're a homeowner, you might be able to get a loan to help with interest payments on your mortgage or other loans you've taken out for your home.

Claiming Universal Credit

You have to fill out an online claim form on GOV.UK. If you need help filling out the form, call the Universal Credit helpline on 0800 **328** 5644 (or textphone 0800 328 1344).Your online claim will be followed by a face-to-face interview.

When you make a claim you will have to agree to certain conditions in return for your benefit. This may be carrying out a training course, or agreeing to the number of hours you'll spend looking for work each week. This could be the case even if you're currently unable to work due to illness. If you don't meet the conditions, your benefit may be reduced.

Your earnings will affect your payments. for more information go to www.gov.uk/universal-credit/how-your-earnings-affect-your-payments.

Caps on all benefits

The government has imposed a cap on the amount of benfits an inividual or couple/family can receive over the course of a year. The cap applies to the total amount that the people in your household get from the following benefits:

- Bereavement Allowance
- Carer's Allowance
- Child Benefit
- Child Tax Credit
- Employment and Support Allowance (unless you get the support component)
- Guardian's Allowance
- Housing Benefit
- Incapacity Benefit
- Income Support
- Jobseeker's Allowance
- Maternity Allowance

- Severe Disablement Allowance
- Widowed Parent's Allowance (or Widowed Mother's Allowance or Widows Pension you started getting before 9 April 2001)

Benefit cap amounts
The amount you get through the benefit cap depends on whether:
- you live inside or outside Greater London
- you're single or in a couple
- your children live with you (if you're single)

If you're in a couple but you do not live together, you'll get the amounts for a single person.

Outside Greater London
The benefit cap outside Greater London is:
- £384.62 per week (£20,000 a year) if you're in a couple
- £384.62 per week (£20,000 a year) if you're a single parent and your children live with you
- £257.69 per week (£13,400 a year) if you're a single adult

Inside Greater London
The benefit cap inside Greater London is:
- £442.31 per week (£23,000 a year) if you're in a couple
- £442.31 per week (£23,000 a year) if you're a single parent and your children live with you
- £296.35 per week (£15,410 a year) if you're a single adult

Who won't be affected?
You might still be affected by the cap if you have any grown-up children or non-dependants who live with you and they qualify for one of the benefits below. This is because they won't normally count as part of your household.

You're not affected by the benefit cap if anyone in your household qualifies for Working Tax Credit or gets any of the following benefits:

- Disability Living Allowance
- Personal Independence Payment
- Attendance Allowance
- Industrial Injuries Benefits (and equivalent payments as part of a war disablement pension or the Armed Forces Compensation Scheme)
- Employment and support allowance if you get the support component
- War Widow's or War Widower's Pension
- War pensions
- Armed Forces Compensation Scheme
- Armed Forces Independence Payment

Tax credits
Working tax credit
Eligibility
Whether you can get Working Tax Credit depends on:
- the hours of paid work you do each week
- your income and circumstances

New Working Tax Credit claims
Working Tax Credit has been replaced by Universal Credit for most people. You can only make a new claim for Working Tax Credit if you get the severe disability premium or got it in the past month and are still eligible for it. If you cannot make a new claim for Working Tax Credit, you may be able to apply for:
- Universal Credit - if you're of working age
- Pension Credit - if you're of Pension Credit qualifying age

Hours you work

Circumstance	Hours a week
Aged 25 to 59	At least 30 hours
Aged 60 or over	At least 16 hours
Disabled	At least 16 hours
Single with 1 or more children	At least 16 hours
Couple with 1 or more children	Usually, at least 24 hours between you (with 1 of you working at least 16 hours)

A child is someone who is under 16 (or under 20 if they're in approved education or training

Exceptions for couples with at least one child
You can claim if you work less than 24 hours a week between you and one of the following applies:

- you work at least 16 hours a week and you're disabled or aged 60 or above
- you work at least 16 hours a week and your partner is incapacitated (getting certain benefits because of disability or ill health), is entitled to Carer's Allowance, or is in hospital or prison

What counts as work
Your work can be:

- for someone else, as a worker or employee
- as someone who's self-employed
- a mixture of the two

If you're self-employed

Some self-employed people are not eligible for Working Tax Credit. To qualify, your self-employed work must aim to make a profit. It must also be commercial, regular and organised. This means you may not qualify if you do not:

- make a profit or have clear plans to make one
- work regularly
- keep business records, such as receipts and invoices
- follow any regulations that apply to your work, for example having the right licence or insurance

If the average hourly profit from your self-employed work is less than the National Minimum Wage, HM Revenue and Customs may ask you to provide:

- business records
- your business plan - find out how to write a business plan
- details of the day-to-day running of your business
- evidence that you've promoted your business - such as advertisements or flyers

Your pay

The work must last at least 4 weeks (or you must expect it to last 4 weeks) and must be paid. This can include payment in kind (for example farm produce for a farm labourer) or where you expect to be paid for the work.

Exceptions

Paid work does not include money paid:

- for a 'Rent a Room' scheme (less than £7,500 or £3,750 for joint owners)
- for work done while in prison
- as a grant for training or studying
- as a sports award

Your income

There's no set limit for income because it depends on your circumstances (and those of your partner). For example, £18,000 for a couple without children or £13,100 for a single person without children - but it can be higher if you have children, pay for approved childcare or one of you is disabled.

What you'll get

You get a basic amount and extra (known as 'elements') on top of this. How much you get depends on things like your circumstances and income. The basic amount is up to £1,960 a year.

Element	Amount
You're a couple applying together	Up to £2,010 a year
You're a single parent	Up to £2,010 a year
You work at least 30 hours a week	Up to £810 a year
You have a disability	Up to £3,090 a year
You have a severe disability	Up to £1,330 a year (usually on top of the disability payment)
You pay for approved childcare	Up to £122.50 (1 child) or £210 (2 or more children) a week

How you're paid

Money is paid directly into your bank or building society account, every week or 4 weeks. You must choose one account if you're a couple. Usually, you're paid from the date of your claim up to the end of the tax year (5 April).

How to claim

As we have stated, Working Tax Credit has been replaced by Universal Credit for most people.You can only make a new claim for Working Tax Credit if you get the severe disability premium or got it in the past month and are still eligible for it. If you cannot make a new claim for Working Tax Credit, you may be able to apply for:

- Universal Credit - if you're of working age
- Pension Credit - if you're of Pension Credit qualifying age

Start a claim

Call HM Revenue and Customs to make a new claim for Working Tax Credit. It can take up to 5 weeks to process a new claim. You can claim after starting a new job, at any time of the year. If you're on benefits (for example Jobseeker's Allowance or Income Support), you can usually start claiming 7 days before you start a new job. You'll be asked for some information and given an estimate of how much you'll get. You may be asked for:

- your National Insurance number (if you have one)
- your income for the last tax year
- details of any benefits you get
- details of any childcare payments
- the number of hours you work per week

HM Revenue and Customs
Telephone: 0345 300 3900
Textphone: 0345 300 3909

Leave and gaps in your employment
You can get Working Tax Credit for periods when you do not work. For example, when you:

- go on maternity leave
- get sick pay
- are in between jobs

You're entitled to the tax credits for a certain period of time providing you qualify.

Circumstance	Period you get tax credits for
You lose or leave your job	For 4 weeks
You're on maternity leave	For the first 39 weeks of your leave
You're on adoption leave	For the first 39 weeks of your leave
You're on paternity leave	For the period of your ordinary paternity leave
You're on additional paternity leave	Up to the equivalent 39th week of your partner's leave
You're off sick	For the first 28 weeks
You're on strike	For the first 10

Circumstance	Period you get tax credits for
	days
You're laid off work	For 4 weeks after you're laid off or the lay off becomes indefinite
You're suspended from work - for example because of a complaint	Usually the period of suspension

Qualifying rules

To qualify, you must:

- have been in paid work
- have worked the right number of hours before you go on leave or the gap happens
- have got Statutory Sick Pay or an equivalent benefit if you were on sick leave

You'll still qualify if you were self employed and you would have been eligible for Statutory Sick Pay or an equivalent benefit if you were not self employed. The equivalent benefits are National Insurance credits (incapacity for work element), Employment and Support Allowance or Income Support (incapacity for work element).

Child tax Credit
Overview

Child Tax Credit has been replaced by Universal Credit for most people. You can only make a new claim for Child Tax Credit if you get the severe disability premium or got it in the past month and are still eligible for it. If your child is 16, you can claim up until 31 August after their 16th birthday. If you cannot make a new claim for Child Tax Credit, you may be able to apply for:

- Universal Credit - if you're of working age
- Pension Credit - if you're of Pension Credit qualifying age

What you'll get

The amount you can get depends on how many children you've got and whether you're:

- making a new claim for Child Tax Credit
- already claiming Child Tax Credit

Child Tax Credit will not affect your Child Benefit. You can only claim Child Tax Credit for children you're responsible for.

What you'll get

The amount you could get depends on when your children were born.

If all your children were born before 6 April 2017

You could get the 'child element' of Child Tax Credit for all of your children. You'll also get the basic amount, known as the 'family element'.

If one or more of your children were born on or after 6 April 2017

You could get the child element of Child Tax Credit for up to 2 children. You might get the child element for more children if exceptions apply. You'll only get the family element if at least one of your children was born before 6 April 2017.

Child Tax Credit rates for the 2018 to 2019 tax year

Element	Yearly amount
The basic amount (this is known as 'the family element')	Up to £545
For each child (this is known as 'the child element')	Up to £2,780
For each disabled child	Up to £3,275 (on top of the child element)
For each severely disabled child	Up to £1,325 (on top of the child element and the disabled child element)

Moving to the UK from the EEA

You must wait 3 months before claiming Child Tax Credit if you arrived in the UK from the EEA on or after 1 July 2014 and do not work. There are some exceptions who will not have to wait 3 months, for example refugees.

You're already claiming Child Tax Credit

How much Child Tax Credit you get depends on your circumstances. You must tell HM Revenue and Customs if your circumstances change.

If your claim started before 6 April 2017

You get:

- the basic amount of Child Tax Credit (known as the 'family element')
- the 'child element' for children born before 6 April 2017
- If you have another child on or after 6 April 2017, you'll usually only get the child element for them if they're the second child you're claiming for.

You might get the child element for more children if exceptions apply.

If your claim started on or after 6 April 2017

You get the child element for up to 2 children. You might get the child element for more children if exceptions apply. You only get the family element if at least one of your children was born before 6 April 2017.

If all your children were born before 6 April 2017

You get the child element for all your children. You also get the basic amount (known as the family element).

Child Tax Credit rates for the 2018 to 2019 tax year

Element	Yearly amount
The basic amount (this is known as 'the family element')	Up to £545
For each child (this is known as 'the child element')	Up to £2,780
For each disabled child	Up to £3,275 (on top of the child element)

Element	Yearly amount
For each severely disabled child	Up to £1,325 (on top of the child element and the disabled child element)

Start your claim

Call HM Revenue and Customs to make a new claim for Child Tax Credit. It can take up to 5 weeks to process a new claim.

Responsibility for a child

You can only claim Child Tax Credit for children you're responsible for. You're usually responsible for a child if:

- they live with you all the time
- they normally live with you and you're the main carer
- they keep their toys and clothes at your home
- you pay for their meals and give them pocket money
- they live in an EEA country or Switzerland but are financially dependent on you

If you share responsibility for a child and you cannot agree who should claim you can both apply. HMRC will decide for you.

If you adopted or fostered a child

You can claim for an adopted or fostered child if you're not getting money from your local council (Health and Social Services Board in Northern Ireland). If you do get money, call HMRC to find out if you can claim.

If you're responsible for a disabled child

You may get extra Child Tax Credits if your child either:

- gets Disability Living Allowance, Personal Independence Payment or Armed Forces independence payment
- is certified blind (or was within 28 weeks of your tax credits claim)

You still qualify if Disability Living Allowance, Personal Independence Payment or Armed Forces Independence Payment stops because the child goes into hospital.

Winter fuel payment

Winter Fuel Payment or Winter Fuel Allowance is an annual payment to help with heating costs, made to households with someone over Pension Credit age. Not heating homes properly puts people at risk of cold-related illnesses such as a heart attack or even hypothermia. The rates for winter fuel payment currently are £200 if you're under 80 and £300 if you're 80 or over.

In winter 2018-19, you will qualify for the payment if you were born before 5 January 1953.

You only need to claim once. After this, you should get it automatically each year, as long as your circumstances do not change. The payment is made directly into your bank account in November or December. For more information you should call the Winter Fuel Payments Helpline on 0800 731 0160.

Cold Weather Payment

Cold Weather Payments are made to eligible people when the weather is very cold. You may get £25 a week when the average temperature has been, or is expected to be, 0°C or below for 7 days in a row (between 1 November and 31 March).

You automatically receive the payment, if you get Pension Credit or certain other means-tested benefits. If you think that you are entitled to a cold weather payment and don't get one contact the Pension Service.

TV licence concessions

You could be entitled to a concession for a TV licence if you are over 75 or someone who is over 75 lives with you. You could also be entitled if you are registered as blind or severely sight impaired or are retired or disabled and live in certain accommodation

The TV licence for your main home doesn't cover you if you have a second home. You will have to buy a separate licence. If you have a licence for your main home, you won't need another if you have a static caravan or mobile home and you don't use the TV at the same time in both places.

You need to apply for a free TV licence if you're 75 or over as it's not given out automatically. You'll need to provide your date of birth and National insurance number (or a photocopy of your passport, driving licence or birth certificate). If you share your house with someone younger than 75, you can still apply for a free licence but it must be in your name. You can apply for your concession by calling 0300 790 6165 or visiting the TV licensing website. Once you have your free TV licence, it will renew automatically annually.

If you apply for a TV licence and you are 74 when you renew your licence you can apply for a short term licence until you are 75.

Concessions for blind and sight-impaired

If you're blind or severely sight-impaired, you can claim a 50% discount on your TV licence. When you apply, you'll need to provide a photocopy of the certificate from your local authority or ophthalmologist confirming your status as well as your TV licence application form and fee. Once you're registered, all your TV licence renewals will be at the concessionary rate.

If you live with someone who is blind or severely-sight impaired, you can get the 50% discount if you transfer the TV licence to the name of that person. You can apply for your concession by calling 0300 790 6165 or visiting the TV licensing website. If you've already paid the TV licence fee but qualify for the blind concession, fill out the TV Licensing online refund form.

Care homes and sheltered housing

You may be entitled to a TV licence concession if you live in a care home or sheltered housing. This licence is called an Accommodation for Residential Care (ARC) licence and it costs £7.50. You'll only need to get one if you watch TV in your own separate accommodation, not if you only watch it in common areas such as a residents' lounge. To qualify, you must be retired and aged 60 or over or disabled and live in accommodation which is eligible. If you think you qualify, contact the warden, staff or managing authority where you live. They will apply for one for you.

If you've already paid your full licence fee and now qualify for an ARC licence, ask your care home manager to help you apply for a refund. If you have questions about the ARC licence, phone TV licensing on 0300 790 6071 or visit the TV licensing website.

Bereavement allowance

Bereavement benefits include:

- o Bereavement Payment - a one-off lump sum you claim when your spouse or civil partner dies
- o Widowed Parent's Allowance if you have dependent Bereavement Allowance if you don't have dependent children

Bereavement benefits are paid to widows, widowers or the surviving partner of a civil partnership. You can get a bereavement benefit if your husband, wife or civil partner died on or after 9 April 2001. If you are a man whose wife died before this date, you may still be able to get some benefit.

You can get a bereavement benefit if you were legally married to your husband or wife who has now died. You can also get a bereavement benefit if you and your same-sex partner who has died registered a civil partnership.

You can't get any of the bereavement benefits if you were divorced from your husband or wife when they died, or you and your civil partner had dissolved your civil partnership. You are also excluded from claiming bereavement benefits if you remarry, or register another civil partnership. If you are getting a bereavement benefit when you remarry or register another civil partnership, it will stop. Even if you do not remarry or register another civil partnership, you cannot get bereavement benefits if you live with another partner. You can't get bereavement benefits in prison.

Bereavement allowance

You may be able to get a £2,000 Bereavement Payment if your spouse or civil partner died before 6 April 2017. This is a one-off, tax-free, lump-sum payment.

If your spouse or civil partner died on or after 6 April 2017 you may be eligible for Bereavement Support Payment instead.

You may be able to get Bereavement Payment if, when your husband, wife or civil partner died, you were either:

- under State Pension age
- over State Pension age and your husband, wife or civil partner wasn't entitled to a State Pension based on their own national insurance contributions

Additionally, your husband, wife or civil partner must have either:
- paid enough National Insurance contributions
- died because of an industrial accident or disease

When you can't get Bereavement Payment
You can't get Bereavement Payment if any of the following are true:

- you were divorced from your husband, wife or civil partner
- you're living with another person as husband, wife or civil partner
- you're in prison

Other bereavement benefits
You may also be eligible for:

- Widowed parents Allowance- if you're bringing up children
- Bereavement Allowance

You don't have to apply more than once - you'll be considered for all bereavement benefits when you apply for one.

If you're abroad
If you've moved abroad contact the International Pension Centre to find out if you can claim.

Bereavement and widows' benefits if you're abroad
Telephone: +44 191 21 87608
Department for Work and Pensions Bereavement and widows' benefits International Pension Centre Tyneview Park Newcastle-upon-Tyne
NE98 1BA

Bereavement Support payment

You may be able to get Bereavement Support Payment if your husband, wife or civil partner died on or after 6 April 2017. You could be eligible if your partner either:

- paid National Insurance contributions for at least 25 weeks
- died because of an accident at work or a disease caused by work

When they died you must have been:

- under State Pension age
- living in the UK or a country that pays bereavement benefits

You cannot claim Bereavement Support Payment if you're in prison.

You'll get a first payment and then up to 18 monthly payments. There are 2 rates.

Rate	First payment	Monthly payment
Higher rate	£3500	£350
Lower rate	£2500	£100

If you get Child Benefit (or if you do not get it but are entitled to it), you'll get the higher rate. If you do not get Child Benefit, you'll get the lower rate unless you were pregnant when your husband, wife or civil partner died.

You must claim within 3 months of your husband, wife or civil partner's death to get the full amount. You can claim up to 21 months after but your payments will be less.

Widowed Parent's Allowance

You may get Widowed Parent's Allowance (WPA) if all the following apply:

- your husband, wife or civil partner died before 6 April 2017 (if your spouse or partner died after this date then you might be able to get bereavement support instead)

- you're under State Pension age

- you're entitled to Child Benefit for at least one child and your late husband, wife or civil partner was their parent

- your late husband, wife or civil partner paid National Insurance contributions, or they died as a result of an industrial accident or disease

You may also claim WPA if you're pregnant and your husband has died, or you're pregnant after fertility treatment and your civil partner has died.

If your husband, wife or civil partner died on or after 6 April 2017 you may be eligible for Bereavement Support Payment instead. You cannot claim WPA if you:

- were divorced from your husband, wife or civil partner when they died

- remarry or are living with another person as if you're married to them or as if you've formed a civil partnership

- were over State Pension age when you were widowed or became a surviving civil partner – you may be able to get extra State Pension

- are in prison

What you'll get

The amount you get is based on how much your late husband, wife or civil partner paid in National Insurance contributions. The maximum Widowed Parent's Allowance (WPA) is £117.10 a week.

If your husband, wife or civil partner died as a result of an industrial accident or disease, you may claim WPA even if they did not pay National Insurance contributions. You can get WPA until you stop being entitled to Child Benefit, unless you reach State Pension age first.

If your WPA ends within 52 weeks of your husband, wife or civil partner's death, you may be able to get Bereavement Allowance for the rest of the 52 weeks.

Effect on other benefits

Once you get WPA, payments may change if you're getting any of the following:

- Income support
- Incapacity Benefit
- Jobseeker's Allowance
- Carer's Allowance
- Employment and Support Allowance
- Universal Credit

Widow's pension

The widow's pension, awarded to widows over age 45, was replaced by the bereavement allowance in 2001. The bereavement allowance is given to widows, widowers or surviving civil partners over age 45 until they reach state pension age. It is paid for up to 52 weeks.

This benefit only applies to people whose partner's died before 6 April 2017. If they died on or after this date, they could qualify for bereavement support payment. The amount you'll get depends on your age at the time of your partner's death, and the overall level of their National Insurance contributions, as the table below shows.

It also depends on your age when your partner dies. The younger you are, the less you'll get. The rates in 2018/19 are as follows:

AGE WHEN SPOUSE DIES	WEEKLY ALLOWANCE
45	£35.13
46	£45.33
47	£51.52
48	£59.72
49	£67.92
50	£76.12
51	£84.31
52	£92.51
53	£100.71
54	£108.90
55 UNTIL STATE PENSION AGE	£117.10

Am I eligible for bereavement allowance?

These are the criteria for claiming bereavement allowance:

- You were aged 45 or over when your partner died.
- You're under state pension age.
- Your partner paid National Insurance contributions, or died in an industrial accident or disease
- You aren't raising children.
- You haven't remarried/joined a civil partnership.
- You aren't living with another person as if you're married/in a civil partnership with them.
- You're not in prison.

Payments for funeral expenses

If you have to pay for a funeral for your partner, a close relative or friend, you may be able to claim a funeral payment from the Social Fund. Partners include lesbian, gay and heterosexual partners, whether you were married, in a civil partnership or living together. To get a funeral payment, you must be getting Income Support, income-based Jobseeker's Allowance, income-related Employment and Support Allowance, Pension Credit, Universal Credit or Housing

Benefit. Some people getting Child Tax Credit or Working Tax Credit may also be entitled to a funeral payment.

Financial help if your husband, wife or civil partner was in the Armed Forces

If your husband, wife or civil partner died as a result of serving in the Armed Forces, you may be able to get financial help from the Service Personnel and Veterans Agency (SPVA). It does not matter whether your husband, wife or civil partner died during active service or not, as long as the death was caused by service in the Armed Forces. You may get a War Widow's or War Widower's pension, or a guaranteed income payment (based on your spouse or civil partner's earnings), depending on when the injury, illness or death was caused.

For information on benefits arising from work related injuries and illnesses see Chapter 4 Employment Rights.

****

Ch. 3

The Criminal Injuries Compensation Scheme 2012

The Criminal Injuries Compensation Scheme is a government funded scheme designed to compensate blameless victims of violent crime in Great Britain. The Criminal Injuries Compensation Authority (CICA), administer the Scheme and decide all claims.The rules of the Scheme and the value of the payments awarded are set by Parliament and are calculated by reference to a tariff of injuries.

You do not need a paid representative such as a solicitor or claims management company to apply for compensation. Free independent advice should be available from Victim Support or other charitable organisations. Victim Support is an independent national charity for people affected by crime and gives free and confidential support, and practical help to victims and witnesses of crime. This can include helping you with your claim, although they cannot provide legal advice. You can contact them by:

o telephoning the Victim Support line on 0808 16 89 111 (England and Wales) or 0800 160 1985 (Scotland);
o visiting their website at www.victimsupport.org.uk or www.victimsupportsco.org.uk; or
o emailing supportline@victimsupport.org.uk or
o info@victimsupportsco.org.uk

You can also get advice from your local Citizens Advice service, a law centre, or from a welfare rights organisation. If you belong to a trade union, they may be able to help.

Paid representation and other help

If you choose paid representation you will have to pay these costs yourself. Where someone is representing you on a 'no-win no-fee' basis this usually means that they will keep a share of your payment to cover their fees. You can also ask a friend or a relative to represent you and help you make a claim.

Payments available from the Scheme

Claims can be considered for the following:

- o   mental or physical injury following a crime of violence;
- o   sexual or physical abuse;
- o   loss of earnings - where you have no or limited capacity to work as the direct result of a criminal injury;
- o   special expenses payments - these cover certain costs you may have incurred as a direct result of an incident. You can only ask them to consider special expenses if your injuries mean you have been unable to work or have been incapacitated to a similar extent for more than 28 weeks;
- o   a fatality caused by a crime of violence including bereavement payments, payments for loss of parental services and financial dependency; and funeral payments.

The Hardship Fund

If your injuries are not serious enough to fall within the tariff of injuries, the Government has introduced a Hardship Fund. The Hardship Fund provides temporary relief from financial hardship to very low paid workers who are temporarily unable to work because they have been a victim of a violent crime. The fund only applies to injuries sustained in England and Wales. For more information, you should contact the Victim Support line on 0845 3030 900.

Making an application for payment

The Compensation Scheme may ask for evidence that you have:

- o considered if it was possible to claim compensation from your assailant and pursued this if there was a chance of success;
- o asked your employer about damages or insurance entitlements; and
- o applied for all benefits to which you may be entitled.

You may still be eligible for an award under the Scheme even if your assailant is not known, or is not convicted.

You must apply as soon as it is reasonably practicable for you to do so. If you were an adult at the time of the incident, this should normally not be later than two years after it occurred. The limit can only be extended where:

- o due to exceptional circumstances an application could not have been made earlier; and
- o the evidence provided in support of the application means that it can be determined without further extensive enquiries by a claims officer.

The decision will be based on the 'balance of probabilities' which is different from a criminal court which decides on the basis of 'beyond reasonable doubt'. The scheme do not need to wait for the outcome of a criminal trial if there is already enough information to make a decision on your case.

If you wish the scheme to consider your application more than two years from the date of the incident you will need to provide evidence that shows why this application could not have been made earlier. You must also be able to provide supporting evidence for your claim that means that the claims officer can make a decision without further extensive enquiries.

Time limit for applicants under 18 years of age on the date of the incident

Special provision is made in the Scheme if you were under 18 at the time of the incident. Although they will consider later applications from you in those circumstances, it is best if you apply as soon as possible. If you are not able to make your own application, your parent or guardian can apply on your behalf. If an application is made close to the time of the incident it will be easier for you to provide evidence that you were injured as the result of a crime of violence.

If the incident or period of abuse was reported to the police before you turned 18, and no-one made a claim on your behalf, you can make a claim up until the day of your 20th birthday. If the incident or period of abuse took place before you turned 18, but was not reported to the police at the time, you can apply within two years from you reporting the incident or abuse to the police. If you wish the scheme to extend these periods for applying you will also need to provide them with evidence that shows why the application could not have been made earlier.

You can apply for compensation online. If you have no access to online services or need help to complete your application, the Customer Service Centre advisors on 0300 003 3601 can help.

Applying on behalf of children

If you are the parent, or person with parental responsibility for a child, you can complete an application on their behalf. You will be asked to provide your details and proof of your relationship to the child.

Applying on behalf of an adult who cannot apply themselves

If you have the authority to act on behalf of a person who lacks the capacity to make their own application, you can apply on their behalf. The scheme will seek evidence that you are entitled to act on their behalf.

They may also need you to obtain medical evidence that the person you are representing lacks capacity, or is 'incapable by reason of mental disorder', within the meanings of the Mental Capacity Act 2005 (England and Wales) or Adults with Incapacity (Scotland) Act 2000.

If the person does not already have someone who is legally appointed to act on their behalf, then you could consider applying to the Court of Protection in England and Wales for the appointment of a deputy or for a single order or, in Scotland, to the Sheriff Court for the appointment of a financial welfare guardian or for an intervention order. There is more information at www.publicguardian.gov.uk (England and Wales) or www.publicguardian-scotland.gov.uk (Scotland).

If you are injured outside Great Britain

If you are a United Kingdom (UK) resident and were injured as a result of a crime of violence in another country which is part of the European Union (EU) the scheme can help you apply for compensation from that country. You should call the EU Assistance Team on 0300 003 3061 or email eucat@cica.gsi.gov.uk. Details of compensation schemes in other countries can be found on the EU Judicial website

If you were injured outside the EU, you may be able to apply under a similar scheme operated by the country concerned. You should contact the Foreign and Commonwealth Office for more information. Details can be found on www.gov.uk.

If you were injured in Northern Ireland, you should contact Compensation Services at:

Albany House, 73-75 Great Victoria Street, Belfast BT2 7AF
Phone: 028 9024 3133

If you were ordinarily resident in the UK and you were injured outside the UK in a terrorist attack, you may be able to claim under the Victims of Overseas Terrorism Compensation Scheme. See the compensation scheme website for more information at www.gov.uk.

The Criminal Injuries Compensation Scheme at ww.gov.uk offers detailed information about claiming for compensation and the criteria involved.

****

Chapter 4

Carers and Help For Carers

In chapter 2, we looked at the range of benefits available to disabled people, including Carers Allowance.

In this chapter, we will look at the all important role of a carer in the life of a disabled person. This section, although meant for carers, will also be of benefit to a disabled person who wishes to know more about the caring profession and what this entails.

What is a Carer?

A carer is anyone who cares, unpaid, for a friend or family member who due to illness, disability, a mental health problem or an addiction cannot cope without their support. The causes of someone taking on caring responsibilities include:

- o   Serious physical illness
- o   Long-term physical disability
- o   Long-term neurological conditions
- o   Mental health problems
- o   Dementia
- o   Addiction
- o   Learning difficulties

The variety of tasks that a carer fulfils is diverse. They can include practical household tasks such as cooking, cleaning, washing up, ironing, paying bills and financial management, personal care such as bathing, dressing, lifting, administering medication and collecting prescriptions and emotional support.

Although the distinction is often made between a full-time or part-time carer, there is not a minimum time requirement or age restriction that "qualifies" someone as being more or less of a carer. If you provide care and support to an adult friend or family member, you may be eligible for support from your local council. Examples might be someone suffering from dementia or mental illness.

This support could include being offered money to pay for things that make caring easier. Or the local authority might offer practical support, such as arranging for someone to step in when you need a short break. It could also put you in touch with local support groups so you have people to talk to.

The Care Act 2014

The Care Act 2014, which was given Royal assent in May 2014, makes carer's assessments more widely available to people in caring roles. Local authorities now have a legal duty to assess any carer who requests one or who appears to need support. If you are a carer and you need some support, you should get in touch with the council covering the area where the person you care for lives. The council will provide you with information and advice about how the assessment will work.

Essentially, a Carer's assessment is a discussion between you and a trained person either from the council or another organisation that the council works with. The assessment will consider the impact the care and support you provide is having on your own wellbeing, as well as important aspects of the rest of your life, including the things you want to achieve day-to-day. It must also consider other important issues, such as whether you are able or willing to carry on caring, whether you work or want to work, and whether you want to study or do more socially. The assessment can be carried out face-to-face, over the telephone or online.

Eligibility for care and support services

A carer's assessment looks at the different ways caring affects your life, and works out how you can carry on doing the things that are important to you and your family. It covers your caring role, your feelings about caring, your physical, mental and emotional health, and how caring affects your work, leisure, education, wider family and relationships. Your physical, mental and emotional wellbeing should be at the heart of this assessment.

When the assessment is complete, the local authority will decide whether your needs are "eligible" for support from the local authority. After the assessment, they will write to you about their decision and give you reasons to explain what they have decided. If you have eligible needs, your council will contact you to discuss what help might be available. If you do not have needs that are eligible, your council will give you information and advice, including what local care and support is available. This could include, for example, help from local voluntary organisations.

Before the assessment

If you have arranged to have a carer's assessment of your needs, give yourself time to think about your role as a carer. You should consider:

○ whether you want to continue being a carer
○ if you were prepared to continue, what changes would make your life easier
○ if there is any risk that you will not be able to continue as a carer without support
○ whether you have any physical or mental health problems, including stress or depression, which make your role as a carer more difficult
○ whether being a carer affects your relationships with other people, including family and friends

- if you are in paid work, whether being a carer causes problems at your work (such as often being late)
- if you like more time to yourself so that you can have a rest or enjoy some leisure activity
- if you like to do some training, voluntary work or paid work

When your carer's assessment is done, you can then consider:

- whether to be a carer at all
- how much care you are willing to provide
- the type of care you are willing to provide

It is vital that the assessment considers whether the role of a carer is affecting your health or safety. Carers sometimes take on physical tasks, such as lifting and carrying, which can cause long-term health problems. Others can find that the stress of the role can lead to depression or other mental health problems. In some cases, safety can be an issue; for instance, because of the behaviour of the person they look after.

- During your assessment, explain any mental or physical health problems you are experiencing. Social services will consider all aspects of your health and safety, including caring tasks that might put your health or wellbeing at risk.

One of the most important parts of the carer's assessment will be a discussion about your wishes concerning paid work, training or leisure activities. The local authority must consider the support you may need if you want to stay in your paid job or return to paid work. They must also consider the support you may need if you want to continue or start studying or training.

If you are looking after someone, the local authority will consider a broad range of issues that can affect your ability to provide care as part of their assessment of your needs. When assessing your needs, social services must consider whether your role as a carer is sustainable. The assessment is about your needs and therefore you should:

- o have a reasonably detailed discussion about all the matters relevant to you
- o have the assessment in private if you want to, at a convenient time and place for you
- o get relevant information, including about welfare benefits you could claim and details of other services
- o have a chance to identify the outcomes that you want; any services should be appropriate for you and meet your needs
- o be given flexibility and innovation in identifying services that may meet your needs
- o have an opportunity to give feedback about the assessment
- o be told about any charges before services are arranged

After your assessment, you and the local authority will agree a support plan, which sets out how your needs will be met. This might include help with housework, buying a laptop to keep in touch with family and friends, or becoming a member of a gym so you can look after their own health.

Your support plan should consider whether your situation is likely to change, but you may want to contact social services and ask them to reassess you if this happens.

Parent carer assessments

If you are a parent of a disabled child aged under 18, your child can be assessed by the local authority under law relating to the needs of children in the Children and Families Act 2014. You will also be assessed as part of that process because social services will look at the needs of the family as a whole. This is often referred to as a "holistic" assessment.

The assessment should take into account detailed information about your family, including:

- o the family's background and culture
- o your own views and preferences
- o the needs of any other children you have
- o The assessment is not a test of your parenting skills, but should be a sensitive look at any difficulties the family has as a whole, with a view to considering what support or services are needed.

A care plan should be drawn up that would include services to benefit both you and your disabled child. For example, there could be adaptations to the home, help with bathing or regular respite breaks to ensure you get the rest you need. You could also choose to have a direct payment so that you can buy in your own services for your child.

Hospital discharge and NHS continuing care

You might have a carer's assessment or a review of your support plan if the person you care for has been in hospital and is being discharged.

As well as care and support organised by the council, some people are also eligible to receive help from the NHS. This help may be a nursing service for people who are ill or recovering at home after leaving hospital. It could include things like changing the dressings on wounds or giving medication. If you are eligible for this kind of help, a health professional such as your GP or community nurse should be able to tell you.

In exceptional circumstances, where an adult has a complex medical condition and substantial ongoing care needs, the NHS provides a service called NHS continuing healthcare. NHS continuing healthcare provides care and support in a person's home, care home or hospice.

****

.

Chapter 5

Options for Care-Paying for Care Homes

In this chapter, we will cover the range of issues covering care homes and the decision to move into a care home. Whether or not you need care home provision will depend on a range of factors, not least the extent of your disability. One of the first and most important options you will have to consider when choosing residential care is whether you need the care home to provide nursing care, or just standard personal care.

There are a variety of options available, from permanent care homes for older people, homes for younger adults with disabilities, and homes for children. Care homes may be privately owned or run by charities or councils. Some will be small care homes based in home-like domestic dwellings, while others will be based in large communal centres.

Options for care before choosing a care home
Going into a care home is a major commitment– it involves changing where you live and potentially committing to paying a considerable amount of money for your ongoing accommodation and care needs. Before you decide to move to a care home, you should think about other options, including:

o   home care
o   help to live independently at home
o   a "shared lives" or "adult placement" scheme – usually suitable for the needs of younger disabled adults (aged 18 to 64)

You should also consider alternatives such as "extra care" housing schemes or warden-controlled sheltered accommodation. These options offer independence with an increased level of care and support.

Personal care or nursing care?

Care homes for older people may provide personal care or nursing care. A care home registered to provide personal care will offer support, ensuring basic personal needs are taken care of. A care home providing personal care only can assist you with meals, bathing, going to the toilet and taking medication, if you need this sort of help.

Some residents may need nursing care, and some care homes are registered to provide this. These are often referred to as nursing homes. For example, a care home might specialise in certain types of disability or conditions such as dementia.

Care homes for adults aged 18 to 65

There are also residential care homes that provide care and support for younger adults with, for example, severe physical disabilities, learning disabilities, brain injury resulting from an accident, or mental health problems.

They can care for adults with more than one condition, and some homes will have expertise in providing care for adults with alcohol or drug dependency. These care homes may offer permanent residence or provide care for a temporary period.

Residential care for children and adolescents

Some care homes specialise in providing residential care for children with physical disabilities, learning disabilities or emotional problems. Residential special schools focus on education and provide teaching on-site. In some cases, care homes for children offer "transition" support for young people until they reach their early 20s.

The choice of care home to suit your needs

The law says that where the local authority is funding accommodation, it must allow a person entering residential care to choose which care home they would prefer, within reason. Social services must first agree the home is suitable for your needs and it would not cost more than you would normally pay for a home that would meet those needs.

Very importantly, local authority assistance with the cost of residential care is means-tested. You are free to make your own arrangements if you can afford the long-term cost. However, it is worth asking the local authority for a financial assessment, because it might pay some or all of your care costs.

In the financial assessment, the local authority can only take into account income and assets you own. The local authority cannot ask members of your family to pay for the basic cost of your care. If you choose a care home that costs more than the local authority usually expects to pay for a person with your needs, you may still be able to live in the care home if a relative or friend is willing and able to pay the difference between what the local authority pays and the amount the care home charges – this is known as a "top-up" fee.

However, if their situation changes and they are no longer able to pay the top-up, the local authority may have no obligation to continue to fund the more expensive care home place and you may have to move out. It is worth thinking about this potentially difficult situation when deciding on care home options.

The value of your home must not be included in the local authority's means-testing until 12 weeks after you've confirmed that the care home placement will be permanent.

It is worth now looking at the Care Act 2014, which has radically shaken up the funding of care homes, and many other areas.

The Care Act 2014

The Care Act 2014 came into force on 1st April 2015 along with a range of new supporting regulations and a single set of statutory guidance, which, taken together, describe how the Act should be applied in practice. The aim of the change is to simplify and modernise the system, which had become very complex and also to create a new approach to charging. The Care Act 2014 came into force in two stages, in April 2015 and April 2016. Some of the key changes introduced in 2015 were:

o The promotion of individual well-being as an overarching principle within all the activities of a local authority including: assessment, eligibility, prevention, means testing and care and support planning.

o New national eligibility criterion for both the adult requesting services and their carer(s) leading to rights to services and based around the well-being principle. The previous four local eligibility levels have now become one, set at approximately the previous 'substantial' level. Carers now have an absolute right to have their assessed, eligible, support needs met for the first time; they have a slightly different eligibility criterion to the service user, but are subject to the same means test rules.

o A person-centred, outcomes-focused, approach to assessing and meeting needs. Local authorities must consider how to meet each person's specific needs rather than simply considering what existing service they will fit into. They must also consider what someone wants/needs to achieve or do and the effect on them of any difficulties they are having.

o   The whole system is now administered via personal budgets and based on the principles of the personalisation policy that has been developed over the past few years.

o   A 'right to request' service provision for a fee where someone with eligible needs is found to be a self-funder (must pay the whole cost of a service) in the means test. This right does not exist for care home provision.

o   New local authority 'market shaping' duties to ensure adequate, diverse, good quality, local service provision.

o   The duty to prevent, reduce and delay the need for services and also related duties to integrate care with the NHS where this benefits a service user.

o   A lifetime care cost cap (set at £72,000 in 2016) above which the State will meet the cost of paying a person's eligible social care needs. The national cap will be reviewed every five years. (This cap has been dropped)

o   The introduction of care accounts, which will require a local authority to track a person's personal expenditure towards meeting their eligible social care needs, towards the new care cost cap –based on the amount set out in their personal budget. Each account will be adjusted annually in line with the national rise in average earnings. Some local authorities may start to assess for care accounts ahead of the April 2016 start date to avoid capacity issues.

o   An increased upper capital limit from £23,250 to £27,000 for non-residential care and support. This includes sheltered accommodation and supported living schemes, which are treated differently to care homes in the means test rules.(At the time of writing 2019 it is still capped at £23,750).

o   An increased tariff income/lower capital limit from £14,250 to £17,000. You should be allowed to keep capital below this level. (Still £14,250) o   Independent personal budgets for those people with assessed, eligible, needs but who have capital in excess of the upper threshold and who are meeting the cost of their care and support themselves. This is a choice that will be available to enable payments to be noted in the person's care account.

There are a wide range of support services that can be provided to help you stay in your own home and also to assist your carer if you have one. Services could include: domiciliary (home) carer and personal assistants; meals delivered at home; day centre attendance and respite care; live-in care services; rehabilitation services; sheltered accommodation and supported living; shared lives services; other housing options; community support; counselling; direct payment support organisations; information, brokerage and advice services1. Other forms of assistance could include the provision of specialist disability equipment, adaptations to your home, community alarms and other types of assistive technology.

There are certain fundamental rules that local authorities must abide by. Charges should not reduce the income that a person has left below a set level. If a person is 60 or over, this is the Pension Credit Guarantee credit level plus a buffer which is dependant where you live in the UK, for example 25% in England and 35% in Wales. The assessment should be based only on your income and generally not that of your partner or anyone else. If you feel that you are paying too much for your care services then you have the right to ask the local authority to review your financial assessment.

How the care is paid for
Either the local authority will pay you direct in cash for your services or, if you so desire, you can ask the local authority to arrange and pay for the care. The Government has also introduced a new scheme called Individual Budgets, arising out of the Care Act

2014, which are similar to Direct Payment, so you receive a cash sum, but it covers a wide range of services so it includes, for example, help towards a warden in sheltered housing. The aim of cash payments is to put the individual in more control of the services that they buy. Obviously, this may not be suited to everyone and some people will be more reliant on the local authority to provide and pay for services.

Other benefits available

There are other benefits available such as personal independence payment (replacing Disability Living allowance for those up to age 64) or if you are over 65 Attendance Allowance. These benefits are tax-free and are not means tested. If you are a carer, you will also have the right to a free needs assessment to pay for extra levels of need.

The care plan devised by the local authority might for example recommend that someone be paid for sitting with a relative whilst you have a few hours off, or respite care (where the disabled person moves temporarily into a care home). You will be expected to pay for these services un

Important considerations when making a decision

If you do decide to enter some form of care home, there are a number of things that you can do to ensure that the care home that you have chosen is suitable for you and is well run. You should check the most recent inspection report to see how well the care home is doing and if there is anything of concern. You can get inspection reports by searching for the care home on the Care Quality Commission website or Ofsted for children's care homes. Also, consider the location of a care home, is it near family and friends, are there shops, leisure or educational facilities in the area? Other things to consider are:

- Is the area noisy, is the care home focused on the residents' individual needs, or do they insist that residents adapt to their routine?
- What arrangements are there for visitors?
- Can residents come and go as they please, as far as it is safe to do so?
- Are staff able to help residents to go out?
- Are outings arranged? What involvement would you have in the care home?
- How would you communicate with staff?
- Are there any support groups or regular meetings?
- If safety and security are issues, what arrangements or supervision can the care home provide?
- Will the care home meet your specific religious, ethnic, cultural or social needs? Will the correct diet be provided?
- Will the right language be spoken? Will there be opportunities to participate in religious activities? Do they allow pets?

Choosing accommodation may be a lifelong decision, so you may want to think about planning for end of life care at the same time. You might also want to check what people who have used the care home say about it from online feedback and review services, such as those put together on NHS Choices. Ask for a temporary stay in the care home before you decide. Temporary stays in care homes can also be arranged in certain circumstances, such as after a stay in hospital. there are differences between good and bad care homes.

A good care home will:

- offer new residents and their families or carers a guide (in a variety of accessible formats) describing what they can expect while they're living there

- have staff who have worked there for a long time, know the residents well, and are friendly, supportive and respectful
- employ well-trained staff, particularly where specialist care such as dementia nursing is required
- involve residents, carers and their families in decision-making
- support residents in doing things for themselves and maximising their independence
- offer a choice of tasty and nutritious food, and provide a variety of leisure and social activities taking residents' needs into account
- be a clean, bright and hygienic environment that's adapted appropriately for residents, with single bedrooms available
- respect residents' privacy, modesty, dignity and choices
- be accredited under the Gold Standards Framework for end of life care

An unsatisfactory care home might:
- have a code of practice, but not adhere to it
- fail to take into account residents' needs and wishes, with most decisions made by staff
- let residents' care plans become out of date, or fail to reflect their needs accurately
- have staff who enter residents' rooms without knocking, and talk about residents within earshot of other people
- deny residents their independence – for example, by not allowing someone to feed themselves because it "takes too long"
- have staff who don't make an effort to interact with residents and leave them sitting in front of the TV all day
- be in a poorly maintained building, with rooms that all look the same and have little choice in furnishings
- need cleaning, with shared bathrooms that aren't cleaned regularly

If you move into a care home, make sure the management and staff of the home know about your condition, disability and other needs. They may have some of this information already – for example, if the local authority has set up the placement after a care needs assessment.

Moving home can be unsettling at the best of times, so when you move into a care home, it's good to have it planned in advance and have family or friends around you when you move to make you feel more comfortable. You should also:

- o contact the benefits office, if you have one (including disability benefits, as these can be affected by care home stays)

- o make sure other services at your previous address have been notified

- o let friends and family know your know contact details and when you might feel up to receiving visitors

Rights of care home residents

The Care Quality Commission (CQC) is the regulator of health and adult social care in England, whether it's provided by the NHS, local authorities, private companies or voluntary organisations.

Under existing rules, independent healthcare and adult social services must be registered with the CQC. NHS providers, such as hospitals and ambulance services, must also be registered.

The registration of organisations reassures the public when they receive a care service or treatment. It also enables the CQC to check that organisations are continuing to meet CQC standards. Standards for care homes are outlined on the CQC website. These standards are underpinned by regulations governing the quality and safety of services. The regulations are enforceable by law – the CQC can enforce fines, public warnings, or even suspend or close a service if they believe people's basic rights or safety are at risk.

Care home closures

Care homes will sometimes close. This can be because the owner decides not to carry on providing the service in that location (for instance, if they retire), or because the home has been sold or failed to meet legal standards. Proposals to close a care home can obviously cause great distress. If the care home is operated by the local authority, it has to follow a consultation process with residents and families. It may be best to get specialist legal advice in this situation. You can find an appropriate solicitor through the Law Society.

****

Chapter 6

Whilst You Are in Hospital

Information for disabled people going into hospital

If you are disabled and you need hospital treatment, it is important that you inform the hospital about the nature of your disability and the extra support you need. If your local doctor refers you for treatment, they will inform the hospital staff of your needs. You can also discuss your requirements with members of hospital staff when they complete your admission form on your arrival in hospital. The admission form gives hospital staff an idea of how much help you may need during your stay in hospital. You might want to discuss:

- any routines you have
- specialist equipment that the hospital may not be able to provide
- having a carer present with you at certain times
- access to facilities, such as bathrooms and toilets
- using a fixed loop or subtitles for television or radio

Benefits

Before you go into hospital, it is important to notify the relevant benefit authorities. For more information about how a hospital stay will affect your benefits, see GOV.UK website on Financial help if you are disabled.

Consent to treatment

For some procedures, including operations, you will be asked to sign a consent form. For more information, see Consent to treatment. Most people with disabilities wil be asked to give their consent to any treatment in hospitals. However, where people lack capacity to give consent, they will be treated under the Mental Capacity Act.

Where a person clearly lacks the capacity to make decisions at the time they are admitted to hospital, health professionals will make what is called a 'best interests decision' on whether specific treatment is in a person's best interests. Doctors and nurses will weigh up the benefits and risks, including whether the person is likely to regain capacity and regain the ability to give or withhold consent.

Leaving hospital
If you are disabled, staff will arrange transport for you, if necessary, to return home when you leave the hospital. If you have recently become disabled, or have given birth to a disabled child, the hospital will tell local social services so that you get the help you need.

****

Chapter 7

Disabled Children-Maternity and Paternity Rights Generally

In this chapter, we will look at the rights of the disabled child and the rights of their parents, specifically rights whilst either pregnant or after pregnancy, with the emphasis on both of the parents. Pregnancy and maternity is now one of the protected characteristics in the Equality Act 2010 and there is now implied into every woman's term of employment a maternity equality clause (s 73 Equality Act 2010). The Act protects women from direct discrimination (s 13(1)) and indirect discrimination (s 19(1)) in relation to pregnancy and maternity.

Right to maternity leave
When you take time off to have a baby you might be eligible for:

- Statutory Maternity Leave
- Statutory Maternity Pay
- paid time off for antenatal care
- extra help from the government

You may also be eligible to get Shared Parental Leave and Pay.

Employment rights when on leave
Your employment rights are protected while on Statutory Maternity Leave. This includes your right to:

- pay rises
- build up (accrue) holiday
- return to work

Leave

Statutory Maternity Leave is 52 weeks. It's made up of:

- Ordinary Maternity Leave - first 26 weeks
- Additional Maternity Leave - last 26 weeks

You don't have to take 52 weeks but you must take 2 weeks' leave after your baby is born (or 4 weeks if you work in a factory). You may be entitled to take some of your leave as Shared Parental Leave.

Start date and early births

Usually, the earliest you can start your leave is 11 weeks before the expected week of childbirth. Leave will also start:

- the day after the birth if the baby is early
- automatically if you're off work for a pregnancy-related illness in the 4 weeks before the week (Sunday to Saturday) that your baby is due

Change your date for returning to work

You must give your employer at least 8 weeks' notice if you want to change your return to work date.

Pay

Statutory Maternity Pay (SMP) is paid for up to 39 weeks. You get:

- 90% of your average weekly earnings (before tax) for the first 6 weeks
- £145.18 or 90% of your average weekly earnings (whichever is lower) for the next 33 weeks

SMP is paid in the same way as your wages (for example monthly or weekly). Tax and National Insurance will be deducted.

If you take Shared Parental Leave you'll get Statutory Shared Parental Pay (ShPP). ShPP is £145.18 a week or 90% of your average weekly earnings, whichever is lower.

Start date

SMP usually starts when you take your maternity leave. It starts automatically if you're off work for a pregnancy-related illness in the 4 weeks before the week (Sunday to Saturday) that your baby is due.

Statutory Maternity Leave

You qualify for Statutory Maternity Leave if:

- you're an employee not a 'worker'
- you give your employer the correct notice

It doesn't matter how long you've been with your employer, how many hours you work or how much you get paid.

You can't get Statutory Maternity Leave if you have a child through surrogacy - you could get Statutory Adoption Leave and Pay instead.

Statutory Maternity Pay (SMP)

To qualify for SMP you must:

- earn on average at least £116 a week
- give the correct notice
- give proof you're pregnant
- have worked for your employer continuously for at least 26 weeks continuing into the 'qualifying week' - the 15th week before the expected week of childbirth

You can't get SMP if you go into police custody during your maternity pay period. It won't restart when you're discharged.

Early births or you lose your baby

You can still get Statutory Maternity Leave and SMP if your baby:

- is born early

-]is stillborn after the start of your 24th week of pregnancy
- dies after being born

If you're not eligible for SMP
Your employer must give you form SMP1 explaining why you can't get SMP within 7 days of making their decision. You may be eligible for Maternity Allowance instead.

How to claim
Statutory Maternity Leave
At least 15 weeks before your due date, tell your employer when the baby is due and when you want to start your maternity leave. Your employer can ask for this in writing.

Your employer must write to you within 28 days confirming your start and end dates.
Use the maternity planner to work out when you must claim your maternity leave.

Statutory Maternity Pay (SMP)
Tell your employer you want to stop work to have a baby and the day you want your SMP to start. You must give them at least 28 days' notice (in writing if they ask for it) and proof that you're pregnant. Your employer must confirm within 28 days how much SMP you'll get and when it will start and stop. If they decide you're not eligible, they must give you form SMP1 within 7 days of making their decision and explain why.

Proof you're pregnant
You need to give your employer proof of the pregnancy to get SMP. You don't need it for maternity leave. Within 21 days of your SMP start date (or as soon as possible if the baby's born early) give your employer either:

- a letter from your doctor or midwife
- your MATB1 certificate - doctors and midwives will give you this no more than 20 weeks before the due date

You won't get SMP if you don't give your employer proof that the baby is due.

Maternity benefits
Working Tax Credit - this can continue for 39 weeks after you go on maternity leave

Income Support - you may get this while you're not working
You could get a £500 Sure Start Maternity Grant (usually if it's your first child).

If you're not eligible for Statutory Maternity Pay, you could get Maternity Allowance from the government.

Company maternity schemes
You might get more than the statutory amount of leave and pay if your employer has a company maternity scheme. They can't offer you less than the statutory amount.

Extra leave
You could get 18 weeks' unpaid parental leave after the birth - this may be restricted to 4 weeks per year.

Parental leave
Parental leave is a legal right to take time off from work to look after a child or make arrangements for a child's welfare. Employers are not legally required to pay workers taking parental leave, so many do not. However, if you are on a low income, you may qualify for income support while you are on parental leave.

Mothers and fathers qualify for statutory parental leave whether they are biological or adoptive parents.

Parental leave is different to other parenting-related leave arrangements such as maternity, adoption and paternity leave.

Your parenting leave entitlement

Working parents are entitled to take up to 18 weeks' parental leave per child up to their eighteenth birthday. Parental leave can be taken for any reason as long as it's related to the care of your child.

Examples of the way it might be used include:

- spending more time with your child in their early years;
- accompanying your child during a stay in hospital;
- looking at new schools;
- settling your child into new childcare arrangements;
- enabling your family to spend more time together. For example, taking them to stay with grandparents.

If you take less than four weeks' parental leave in one block, you have the legal right to return to your old job. If you take more than four weeks in a block, you are only entitled to return to the job you did before if it is reasonably practicable. If it isn't, your employer must give you a comparable and appropriate job.

You can only take parental leave if you have been continuously employed for not less than a year and have, or expect to have responsibility for the child.

"Responsibility for the child" is a legal term. You will normally have responsibility for the child if you are the mother of the child or the father of the child and you are either married to the mother of the child or your name appears on the birth certificate of the child, having registered jointly with the mother.

Special arrangements

Some employers allow flexibility in the way parental leave is taken. You might, therefore, be able to work reduced hours over a given period, for example, without losing any pay. Or your employer may allow you parental leave even though your child is over the statutory age for you to legally qualify.

Dealing with emergencies

Even if you don't qualify for parental leave, you should be able to get time off to deal with genuine emergencies. You have the right to take a reasonable amount of unpaid time off to deal with certain emergencies involving people you care for. You qualify for "time off for dependents" regardless of how long you have been working for your employer.

Paternity leave and pay

Employees whose partner is having a baby, adopting a child or having a baby through a surrogacy arrangement may be entitled to paternity leave and pay. Workers, while not entitled to paternity leave, may be entitled to receive paternity pay.

What is paternity leave?

Paternity leave is a period of either one or two consecutive weeks that fathers or partners can take off from work to care for their baby or child. It is available to employees who:

- have or expect to have responsibility for the child's upbringing
- are the biological father of the child, the mother's husband or partner (including same sex relationships) **or** the partner of the primary adopter
- have worked continuously for their employer for 26 weeks ending with the 15th week before the baby is due, or the end of the week in which the child's adopter is notified of being

matched with the child (UK adoption), or the date the child enters the UK (overseas adoptions).

Taking paternity leave
Births

An employee must inform their employer no later than the end of the 15th week before the expected week of childbirth that they wish to take paternity leave. They should say when the baby is due, if they're going to take one or two weeks off, and when they expect their paternity leave to start.

An employee can choose for their leave to begin on:
- the day the baby is born
- a certain number of days after the baby is born
- a specific date which is not earlier than when the baby is due.

Paternity leave cannot start before the baby is born and the baby may not arrive on time. An employer should therefore be prepared to flexible with cover arrangements for employees planning to take paternity leave.

Employees will need to complete their paternity leave within 56 days of the actual date of birth of the child.

Adoptions and Surrogacy Arrangements

When adopting, one partner, if they qualify, can take adoption leave as the main adopter and the other may be entitled to paternity leave. A period of paternity leave when adopting a child can start:
- on the date of placement
- an agreed number of days after the date of placement
- on the date the child arrives in the UK or an agreed number of days after (for overseas adoption)
- the day the child is born or the day after for surrogate parents.

In all adoptions, an employee will need to have taken their Paternity Leave within 56 days of the placement date.

Receiving paternity pay

Employees or workers who take time off may be entitled to either Statutory Paternity Pay or Contractual Paternity Pay.

Statutory Paternity Pay

Statutory Paternity Pay will be payable if an employee or worker has been:

- working continuously for one company for at least 26 weeks ending with the 15th week before the expected week of childbirth
- has an average weekly earnings at least equal to the lower earnings limit for National Insurance contributions.

Since April 2018 the rate has been £145.18 per week or 90 per cent of the average weekly earnings, whichever is less.

Contractual Paternity Pay

An employer may choose to offer a rate of pay which is higher than the statutory rate. The amount and the length for which it is paid should be set out in the terms and conditions of employment. Contractual paternity pay cannot be lower than the statutory rate.

Other leave options

An employee may not qualify for paternity leave, or they may want to take some additional time off when the baby is born. In these circumstances an employee could consider the following:

Shared Parental Leave

Give parents more flexibility in how they share the care of their child in the first year following birth or adoption. Eligible parents can exchange part of their maternity or adoption leave for Shared Parental Leave. They can then share this leave with each other in a way that best suit their needs in caring for their child.

Annual leave

An employee could submit an annual leave request to take time off at the time the baby is born. This should be done in accordance with the employer's annual leave policy and the employer would have the right to accept or decline the request depending on business needs.

Unpaid time off

An employee could discuss with their employer whether they could come to an agreement to take unpaid time off. This could only be done if both employee and employer agree to it.

Attending Antenatal or Adoption Appointments
Antenatal classes

Fathers and partners of a pregnant woman are entitled to unpaid time off during working hours to accompany her to two ante-natal appointments. The time off should not exceed 6.5 hours per appointment and should be used to travel to and attend the appointment. If this takes less than 6.5 hours the employee should return to work unless alternative arrangements have been made with their employer.

There is no legal right to paid time off for attending antenatal appointments. However, an employee's contract of employment may entitle them to the time off with pay. If an employee does not want to take unpaid time off, they could request annual leave or ask if they could work the hours at a different time.

The right to two unpaid antenatal appointments also includes employees who will become parents through a surrogacy arrangement if they expect to satisfy the conditions for, and intend to apply for, a Parental Order.

Adoption appointments

The main adopter is able to take paid time off for up to 5 adoption appointments. The main adopter's partner (secondary adopter) is entitled to take unpaid time off for up to 2 appointments.

Still births and sick babies

If the baby is stillborn after the twenty fourth week of pregnancy or if the baby is born alive at any point (even if the baby later passes away) the employee is entitled to full paternity rights if they satisfy the conditions above.

When a baby is born prematurely or with health needs an employee may not want to be thinking about work. An employer should offer appropriate support in these circumstances.

Agency Workers and paternity rights

Agency workers do not usually qualify for paternity leave (unless they are an employee of the agency). However, an agency worker may qualify for paternity pay if they meet the qualifying criteria. If an agency worker qualifies for paternity pay they should write to their agency at least 28 days before they want the payment to begin stating:

- the agency worker's name
- when the baby is due
- when the worker would like the payment to begin
- whether they are requesting one or two weeks pay.

Agency workers can usually choose when to make themselves available for work so may choose to be unavailable for work for a period of time after the baby is born. An agency worker whose partner is pregnant has the right to attend two unpaid antenatal appointments with their partner once they have completed a twelve week qualifying period with one hiring company.

Employment rights during paternity leave

An employee has the right to not be treated less favourably by their employer for taking, or proposing to take, paternity leave. An employee also has the right to return to their own job following a period of paternity leave and their terms and conditions should remain the same.

Annual leave (including Bank Holidays where applicable) continues to accrue during paternity leave and an employee must be able to take this leave at some point during their leave year.

Unfair treatment during, or because of, paternity leave

If an employee feels that they have been treated unfairly because of taking, or proposing to take, paternity leave, they should first consider raising the issue informally. Some issues can be resolved quickly through a conversation with a line manager or other person within the business.

If an informal approach does not work, an employee has the option of raising a formal complaint (also known as a grievance). This should be done in writing and can make the employer aware of how strongly the employee feels about the situation, while also giving the employer the opportunity to resolve it.

As a last resort the employee could consider making a complaint to an Employment Tribunal. There is generally a three month time limit for bringing a claim to Employment Tribunal. However this time limit can be paused if Early Conciliation is taking place.

Shared parental leave and pay

Shared Parental Leave (SPL) enables eligible mothers, fathers, partners and adopters to choose how to share time off work after their child is born or placed for adoption. This could involve returning to work for part of the time and then resuming leave at a later date.

How Shared Parental Leave works

Shared Parental Leave can give parents more flexibility in how they share the care of their child in the first year following birth or adoption. Parents can share up to 50 weeks of leave and up to 37 weeks of pay and choose to take the leave and pay in a more flexible way (each parent can take up to 3 blocks of leave, more if their employer allows, interspersed with periods of work).

Eligible parents can be off work together for up to 6 months or alternatively stagger their leave and pay so that one of them is always at home with their baby in the first year.

Who can apply for Shared Parental Leave?

To trigger the right to SPL for one or both parents, the mother/adopter must:

- have a partner
- be entitled to:
- maternity/adoption leave
- to statutory maternity/adoption pay
- maternity allowance (if not eligible for maternity/adoption leave)
- have curtailed, or given notice to reduce, their maternity/adoption leave, pay or allowance.

A parent who intends to take SPL must:

- be an employee
- share the primary responsibility for the child with the other parent at the time of the birth or placement for adoption
- have properly notified their employer of their entitlement and have provided the necessary declarations and evidence.

In addition, a parent wanting to take SPL is required to satisfy the 'continuity of employment test' and their partner must meet the 'employment and earnings test'.

Continuity of Employment test	Employment and earnings test
The individual has worked for the same employer for at least 26 weeks at the end of the 15th week before the child's expected due date/matching and is still working for the employer at the start of each leave period.	In the 66 weeks leading up to the baby's expected due date/matching date, the person has worked for at least 26 weeks and earned an average of at least £30 a week in any 13 weeks.

Sometimes only one parent will be eligible. For example a self-employed parent will not be entitled to SPL themselves but they may still pass the employment and earnings test so their partner, if they are an employee, may still qualify. If both parents are employees and meet the qualifying requirements then there will be a joint entitlement. The parents will have to decide how to divide the leave entitlement once the mother/adopter has decided to curtail their maternity/ adoption leave.

Shared Parental Pay

From April 2018, Statutory Shared Parental Pay is paid at £145.18 or 90% of an employee's average weekly earnings (whichever is lower). If the mother or adopter curtails their entitlement to maternity/adoption pay or maternity allowance before they have used their full entitlement then Statutory Shared Parental Pay can be claimed for any remaining weeks.

To qualify for Statutory Shared Parental Pay a parent must pass the continuity of employment test and have earned an average salary of the lower earnings limit of £116 for the 8 weeks' prior to the 15th week before the expected due date or matching date. The other parent in the family must meet the employment and earnings test.

How to apply for leave and pay

Having an early and informal discussion can provide an opportunity for both the employee and employer to talk about their preference regarding when Shared Parental Leave is taken. It can also be an opportunity to discuss when any discontinuous leave can be best accommodated if appropriate. If an employee wishes to take Shared Parental Leave they must notify their employer of their entitlement **at least eight weeks before the start** of any Shared Parental Leave starts. It is good practice for an employer to confirm they have received and accept this notification.

Each eligible parent can give their employer up to 3 separate notices booking or varying leave, although each must be given at least eight weeks before the leave is due to start. Each notice can be for a single block of leave, or the notice may be for a pattern of "discontinuous" leave involving different periods of leave. If a parent asks for a continuous block of leave the employer is required to agree to it. However, where the notification is for discontinuous blocks of leave the employer can refuse and require that the total weeks of leave in the notice be taken in a single continuous block. It is therefore beneficial for the employee and employer to discuss and attempt to agree a way in which the different blocks of leave can be taken.

Handling an application for SPL

Depending on the circumstances involved, there are four outcomes available to an employer once they have received, considered and discussed a Shared Parental Leave notification. It is important to note an employer **cannot refuse a notification for continuous leave**.

A) Confirm a continuous leave period or accept a discontinuous leave request.

B) Agree a modification to a leave request (an employee is under no obligation to modify a continuous leave notice and should never be put under any pressure to do so).

C) Refuse a discontinuous leave notification.

D) Whilst it is not good practice and should be avoided, it is possible for an employer to make no response to a leave notification.

For outcomes **C** and **D** above, the employee can withdraw their notification on or before the 15th calendar day after the notification was originally made and it will not count as one of their three notifications. If not, they must take the total amount of leave notified in one continuous block. The employee can choose when this leave period will begin within 19 days of the date the notification was given to the employer but it cannot start sooner than the initial notified start date. If they don't, the leave will begin on the starting date stated in the original notification.

Employers may wish to develop a policy that sets out the rules and procedures for applying for and taking Shared Parental Leave.

Some organisations offer enhanced maternity rights, giving mothers maternity pay above the statutory minimum, for example 26 weeks' full pay followed by 13 weeks SMP. Organisations may wish to "mirror" their maternity enhancements in any Shared Parental Leave policy.

There is no established statutory requirement to mirror occupational maternity schemes when a Shared Parental Leave scheme is established. The important thing is that within a Shared Parental Leave scheme, men and women are treated equally and paid at the same rate in the same circumstances.

New entitlement to Parental Bereavement Leave and Pay

The Government is introducing a new workplace right to Parental Bereavement Leave and Pay for parents who lose a child under the age of 18, including those who suffer a stillbirth from 24 weeks of pregnancy.

The Parental Bereavement (Leave and Pay) Act gained Royal Assent in September 2018. Work is underway to get the Regulations ready to be laid before Parliament in 2019, with the intention that they will apply from the common commencement date of 6 April 2020.

Who will be entitled?

Employed parents who lose a child under the age of 18 (or those who suffer stillbirth from 24 weeks) will be entitled to 2 weeks of Parental Bereavement Leave as a 'day-one' right. Those with at least 26 weeks continuous service at the date of their child's death and earnings above the Lower Earnings Limit will also be entitled to Parental Bereavement Pay, paid at the statutory flat weekly rate of £145.18 (or 90% of average earnings, where this is lower).

The definition of a 'bereaved parent' is guided by the principle that those who are the 'primary carers' of the child should be the focus of the entitlement. The entitlement will apply to the child's 'legal' parents; individuals with a court order to give them day-to-day responsibility for caring for the child; and primary carers who do not have legal status, such as kinship carers. In all cases, eligibility will be based on facts that will be clear to both the employee and their employer in order to minimise confusion.

How can the leave and pay be taken?

Eligible parents will be able to take both the leave and pay as either a single block or one or two weeks, or as two separate blocks of one week of leave and/or pay (taken at different times). The employee will have 56 weeks from the date of their child's death in which to take the entitlement so as to allow parents to take the leave (and pay) at important moments, such as anniversaries, if they wish.

What notices will be required?

No prior notice will be required for leave taken very soon after the death. This will apply for a set number of weeks, in recognition that employees are likely to need to take leave at little or no notice. Employees will, however, be required to tell their employer that they are absent from work – informal notification will be acceptable. If leave is taken at a later point in time, a notice requirement will apply. The proposed notice period is at least one week.

Prior notice will be required for Parental Bereavement Pay irrespective of when the pay is taken. This is in order to give employers time to process the request.

What will the evidence requirements be?

The Government is considering whether employers should be able to request evidence of entitlement to Parental Bereavement Leave where an employee is required to give notice (i.e. where the leave is taken at a later date). Where they do, the Government proposes that this should be in the form of a written declaration that the employee meets eligibility criteria for leave (this is the approach used for Paternity Leave and Pay). This means that employers will not be able to ask parents for evidence of the child's death (e.g. they will not be able to ask for a copy of the death certificate) nor of their relationship with the child. However, when an employee needs to take time off work to grieve very soon after the death of their child, they will not be required to provide a written declaration before going on leave or subsequently. There will be no obligation on employers to ask for this information, and no obligation on employees to provide it (i.e. it will not be part of the eligibility requirements). For Parental Bereavement Pay, a written declaration will always be required from the employee in order to safeguard employers and the Exchequer from potential abuse, as is the case for other family related pay entitlements. The Parental Bereavement (Leave and Pay) Act 2018 applies only to Great Britain. At the current time, no legislation to introduce parental bereavement leave or pay has been introduced in Northern Ireland, therefore, the measure will not apply in Northern Ireland.

Adoption leave and pay
Qualifying employees who have been matched with a child may take up to 52 weeks adoption leave, and may be entitled to 39 weeks of statutory adoption pay. If a couple jointly adopt a child, one may take adoption leave and the other parent may be able to take paternity leave or shared parental leave.

Key points
The main adopter will be able to take paid time off for up to five adoption appointments. The secondary adopter will be entitled to take unpaid time off for up to two appointments. Adoption leave is a "day one" right there is no qualifying period.

Statutory Adoption Pay - the first six weeks will be paid at 90% of the employee's normal earnings. Some surrogate parents will become eligible for adoption leave. Adoption leave may be taken:

- When a child starts living with the employee or up to 14 days before the placement date (UK adoptions).
- When an employee has been matched with a child by a UK adoption agency.

- When the child arrives in the UK or within 28 days (overseas adoption).

The partner of an individual who adopts, or the secondary adopter if a couple are adopting jointly may be entitled to paternity leave and pay or shared parental leave. Employees must give their employer documentary proof to show that they have the right to paid Statutory Adoption Leave. This is usually a matching certificate from the adoption agency. The adoption agency must be recognised in the UK.

Statutory adoption leave can start either:
- from the date the child starts living with the employee
- up to 14 days before the date the child is expected to start living with the employee.

Employees should tell the employer within seven days of being told that they have been matched with a child, if this is not possible they must tell the employer as soon as possible. Employees who request or take adoption leave are protected against suffering a detriment or unfair dismissal. They have a right to return to the same job after 26 weeks adoption leave and after 52 weeks a suitable alternative job must be found.

Statutory Adoption Pay
Since April 2015, the rate of statutory adoption pay has been £139.58 per week. For the first six weeks the employee will be entitled to 90% of their normal earnings. The following 33 weeks will be paid at the statutory adoption pay rate. Some employers may offer to pay more than this - if they do it may form part of the terms and conditions of the employment contract. From 2 April 2017, the rate went up to be £140.98.

Keep in touch day

Both parties should agree when and how the employer will keep in contact, this may be via email, telephone contact etc. Employees should also agree with their employer if they will work the "keeping in touch" days, these can be used for training days, team events etc.

Up to ten keeping in touch days can be worked, and there is no provision for these days to be paid, this should be agreed between employee and employer. Statutory Adoption Pay may be paid or this may be off set against any contractual pay agreed.

Other benefits available if your child is disabled

Disability Living Allowance and Personal Independence Payment

If you have a disabled child under 16, you may be able to claim a benefit called Disability Living Allowance (DLA) for them. DLA has two components. The mobility component may be paid if your child has problems with getting around, and the care component may be paid if they have care needs which are more than most children of their age.

You cannot get the mobility component for a child under three. There is no age requirement for the care component, but you cannot usually claim it for a baby under three months old. This is because your child must have had care needs or mobility problems for at least three months before they can be entitled to DLA, unless they are terminally ill. It can be difficult to claim DLA for a young child and it may help to get specialist advice.

If your child is 16 or over and on DLA, they will be invited to claim Personal Independence Payment (PIP) instead of DLA, unless they are terminally ill (when they stay on DLA until their award expires). There is more information about the move to PIP on the Contact a Family website.

If your child is 16 or over and doesn't have an existing DLA claim, they will have to claim PIP.

DLA and PIP, claimed for you or your children, do not depend on income so are not affected when you move into or out of paid work.

DLA and PIP are complex benefits. It is advisable to seek personal advice when applying because the claim forms are long and you are more likely to be successful with professional advice.

DLA and PIP are 'passports' to other benefits and services – for example, you may get more Child Tax Credit (see below) if your child receives DLA or PIP.

Child Benefit and Child Tax Credit

You should also be able to claim Child Benefit and Child Tax Credit for your child. You may get more Child Tax Credit if your child gets DLA or PIP, because there is an extra element of Child Tax Credit included in the calculation. Make sure you tell the Tax Credit Office what rate of DLA or PIP your child is getting. In some areas of the country, if you are making a new claim for Child Tax Credit you will be told to claim Universal Credit instead. This also has extra elements for children on DLA or PIP.

Working Tax Credit (WTC)

WTC can be claimed by a lone working parent or a couple in which one or both partners work (see Working Tax Credit). The basic amount you are awarded is tapered off as your income increases. You may also qualify for help with childcare costs (see Childcare element of Working Tax Credit).

If your disabled child is 16 or over and works 16 hours or more, they may be able to claim WTC themselves, as long as they receive DLA or PIP (see Working Tax Credit). You should get advice if you need to make decisions about whether you claim for your child or they claim for themselves (see transition guide). You can't get Child Benefit or Child Tax Credit for a young person who claims WTC.

In some parts of the country, someone making a new claim for Working Tax Credit will be told to claim Universal Credit (UC) instead. You can't get Child Benefit or Child Tax Credit for a young person who claims UC. If you are not sure whether a young person does have to claim UC, get advice, as it can be less generous than Working Tax Credit.

Carer's Allowance
If you are a carer for your disabled child and they get the middle or higher rate care component of DLA, or the daily living component of PIP, you may be able to get Carer's Allowance. If you are thinking of taking up work you may want to consider the effect it may have on your entitlement to Carer's Allowance.

Employment and Support Allowance (ESA)
Over 16s who are not working and would have difficulty working because of illness or disability can claim Employment and Support Allowance (ESA) (see Benefits for disabled adults). The test for ESA can be quite difficult to meet and it is worth getting advice if your child is unsuccessful. Young people claiming DLA/PIP can claim ESA while still in education. However, you can't claim Child Benefit or Child Tax Credit at the same time as your young person claims ESA, so you may need advice about which to claim, or you can research the amounts involved. You can look at the different benefit amounts which would be paid depending on who claims by using an online calculator like the one on the website Turn2Us. Even if your young person claims ESA, you can still be their appointee for the benefit, if that is necessary (that means you would be responsible for making the claim and reporting all changes of circumstances).

In some parts of the country, a young person claiming income-related ESA will be told to claim Universal Credit (UC) instead. You can be an appointee for UC if necessary (it is usually claimed online). You can't claim Child Benefit or Child Tax Credit for a young person who is claiming UC, so you may need advice. UC can be less generous than income-related ESA, for example if your child gets

PIP, and/or is thinking of working, so also get advice if you are not sure if they do have to claim UC.

Direct Payments (DP)

If your disabled child, having been assessed by your local authority, is entitled to services, you can choose to have direct payments (DP) and buy the services yourself. DP are for the stipulated services and are not affected by what you earn.

Disabled Facilities Grant

If your local authority provides a grant to alter your home to suit your disabled child's needs it is not affected by your income.

Housing Benefit and Council Tax Reduction

Housing Benefit and Council Tax Reduction (help with the council tax from your local authority) depend on your income. These benefits also depend on how many dependent children you have and the calculation will be different if your children are on DLA or PIP, so make sure the local authority know about this. In addition, the number of bedrooms allowed for in the Housing Benefit (HB) calculation could be higher if your children are unable to share a room because of disability and they are on DLA or PIP. Again make sure the local authority are aware.

In some areas of the country, if you make a new claim for Housing Benefit, you will be told to claim Universal Credit instead. The same bedroom rules apply.

If you move into work, you may, depending on your income, still be entitled to such help but you need to inform your local authority for the benefits to be recalculated. You can use the calculator at the website www.turn2us.org.uk to check your entitlement.

Family Fund

The Family Fund gives discretionary grants to families with severely disabled children under 18. They have their own definition of 'severely disabled'. The grants are for things not supplied by statutory authorities. Usually the grants are made to families on benefits, but the fund may also be able to help other families on low incomes.

Help with health costs

You can qualify for help with health costs, for example prescriptions and sight tests, if you receive some benefits such as Income Support, Income-based Jobseeker's Allowance, Income-related Employment and Support Allowance, or the Guarantee credit of Pension Credit . Some people on Universal Credit or tax credits may be entitled, and you may also be able to apply for help if you are on a low income. Prescriptions are free for under 16s, and under 19s in full-time education.

****

Chapter 8

Disabled People and Employment and Workplace Rights

This chapter covers the support and training available to help disabled people into work. It also covers employers responsibilities towards disabled people in the workplace.

Entering employment

The role of Jobcentre plus and Disability Employment Advisors

Jobcentre plus is the Department of Work and Pensions organisation providing benefits and services to people of working age. This means age 16 or over. Everyone who claims benefits from Jobcentre Plus is allocated a personal advisor to deal with claims for benefit and help them back into work. Disabled people also have access to a Disability Employment Advisor who provide employment assessment, job seeking advice and assistance with training as well as specialist advice and information. It is important to note that advice and support from a DEA is not dependant on benefits it is available to any disabled person.

Work programmes

There are a number of work programmes managed by 'providers' who are contracted by the government which aim to help people find work and stay in work. They provide activities such as work experience, work trials, help to become self-employed, voluntary work, training and ongoing support. The programmes are mandatory if a person is considered capable of work. Referral to work programmes is normally through Jobcentre Plus. If in receipt of Job Seekers Allowance a person will have to take part in the Work Programme after nine months. If the advisor agrees a person may join earlier than this if they wish. If they receive Employment and Support Allowance the time for entry to a Work Programme will vary depending on an assessment of a person's fitness to work.

Community Work Placement Programme

The Community Work Placement Programme was designed for Jobseeker's Allowance claimants who require further support to obtain and sustain employment following a Work Programme placement. Participants had to undertake work placements for the benefit of the community and work-related activity. This programme was mandatory. It has now been withdrawn.

Work Choice

The work choice programme, which is now closed to new applicants, was aimed at people who were experiencing barriers to work arising from a disability or who were in work but risk losing their job as a result of a disability. Participation is voluntary and usually they must be referred by a Disability Employment Advisor. Work choice consists of two modules, each of which is tailored to their specific needs:

- o Work Entry Support-this is up to six months help with vocational guidance, confidence building, job search advice and other support such as job application skills. In some cases, this support can be for longer than six months;In-Work Support-this is up to 12 months support once a person is in employment. The Work Choice Provider will work with them and their employer to identify the support needed and also help them develop the necessary skills and knowledge to move to unsupported employment;

Work choice was available throughout the UK with the exception of Northern Ireland where there are similar schemes.

Access to Work www.gov.uk/access-to-work

Access to Work is designed to help disabled people overcome any barriers that they may face in obtaining employment and retaining employment. Access to Work provides practical advice and also grants towards extra costs which may be incurred arising from a disability. This advice and support can include special aids and adaptations, or equipment needed for employment, adaptations premises (not new) and equipment, help with travel, help with a support worker, a communicator and, if needed, an interpreter.

Certain types of expenditure are excluded, details of which can be obtained during the application stage. Costs which are the responsibility of the employer, for example costs which are seen as a 'reasonable adjustment' under the Equality Act 2010, are not included. (See below for details of 'reasonable adjustments').

A person will be eligible for help through the Access to Work scheme if they are employed, including as an apprentice, self-employed or unemployed and have a job to start and they are disabled. Access to Work defines disability as in the Equality Act 2010 (see introduction) but also includes impairments and health conditions that are only evident in the workplace.

Access to Work also provides help to people with mental health conditions and learning difficulties. The service provides a wide range of support for a period of six months for people with mental health conditions, including work focussed mental health support tailored to the individual, assessment of an individuals needs, a personalised support plan, advice and guidance to employers and the identification of reasonable adjustments needed in the workplace.

*

How much support can a person receive?

If a person has been in a job for less than six weeks, are self-employed or are about to start work, Access to Work will cover 100% of approved costs. If they have been employed for six weeks or more when they apply for help, Access to Work will pay only some of the costs of support, called 'cost sharing' which is dependant on the number of employees in an organisation. The funding agreements can last up to three years with an annual review.

You can apply for access to work online or by phone, 0800 121 7459. Normally there will be a telephone interview by an advisor to assess eligibility.

Training

There are numerous government training programmes designed to help prepare people for work. Details can be found from a nearest Jobcentre Plus office. There are many courses available designed to help disabled people. Contact a disabled employment advisor at the local Jobcentre Plus office or ring the National Careers Service Helpline 0800 100 900 or Skills Development Scotland 0800 917 8000.

Benefits while training

DLA and PIP are not usually affected if training is undertaken or if a person gets a training allowance. However, DLA care component and PIP daily living component will not usually be paid for any days that a person stays in a care home to attend a residential training programme. The residential training programmes aim to help long-term unemployed adults overcome disability related barriers to employment.

Advice concerning benefits entitlement, such as Universal Credit Income Support, Jobseeker's allowance and Employment and Support Allowance and how they are affected by training, can be obtained from a local Jobcentre Plus.

When a person is in work

Disability and employers responsibilities
It's against the law for employers to discriminate against anyone because of a disability. The Equality Act 2010 protects everyone and covers areas including:
- o application forms
- o interview arrangements
- o aptitude or proficiency tests
- o job offers
- o terms of employment, including pay
- o promotion, transfer and training opportunities
- o dismissal or redundancy
- o discipline and grievances

Reasonable adjustments in the workplace
Those employees with disabilities share the same employment rights as other workers with the addition of some other rights as stated within the Equality Act 2010. Within this act, employers are expected to make 'reasonable adjustments' within the workplace with regard to access and facilities for disabled members of staff. The provisions set out in the Equality Act apply to every employer, no matter the size or industry (except the armed forces). It is worth noting that the reasonable adjustment requirements are not necessary to carry out in anticipation or only in case an employer gains a disabled employee. The adjustments need only be carried out once a disabled person is employed or applies for a role within the company.

To comply with the Equality Act 2010, an employee must suffer from severe or long-term impairments. Impairments of disabled employees include:
- o Physical impairments - mobility disabilities
- o Mental impairments - long term (12 months plus) mental illnesses or learning disabilities

o   Sensory impairments - visual or hearing impairments.

What are reasonable adjustments?

The Equality Act states employers have a duty to amend the workplace in order to accommodate both disabled employees and/or applicants for job roles. These adjustments are in order to avoid disabled people being at a disadvantage when applying for a job or indeed working within an organisation. Reasonable adjustments can vary and cover areas from working arrangements to physical changes around the workplace.

Adjusted working arrangements may be flexible working hours to allow disabled employees to be able to meet their employment requirements, or amendments being made to workplace equipment, adapting it to suit employee's capabilities.

If a physical feature within the workplace creates a disadvantage for a disabled employee, steps must be taken to amend or remove the obstruction. Physical adjustments can include changes such as:

o   The addition of a ramp rather than steps to access buildings.
o   Providing disabled toilet facilities need to provided to accommodate those that need them.
o   The widening of doorways to allow for wheelchair access.
o   Repositioning door handles and/or light switches etc to ensure they can be reached.

In some cases, an employer may need to provide disabled employees with extra help through an aid to ensure that the disabled employee is not at any disadvantage against other workers. This aid may be in form of specialist or adapted equipment, such as special computer keyboards or telephones.

With regard to a disabled person applying for a job, an employer does not necessarily need to make the physical adjustments before the interview. It will suffice that an easily accessible location and necessary support and assistance for the applicant to get there is provided. If the applicant is then employed, the employer must consider the other adjustments mentioned above.

Recruitment

An employer who is recruiting staff may make limited enquiries about a person's health or disability. They can only be asked about their health or disability:

- o to help decide if they can carry out a task that is an essential part of the work
- o to help find out if they can take part in an interview to help decide if the interviewers need to make reasonable adjustments for them in a selection process
- o to help monitoring
- o if they want to increase the number of disabled people they employ
- o if they need to know for the purposes of national security checks

A person may be asked whether they have a health condition or disability on an application form or in an interview. Thought needs to be given as to whether the question is one that is allowed to be asked at that stage of recruitment.

Redundancy and retirement

A person can't be chosen for redundancy just because they are disabled. The selection process for redundancy must be fair and balanced for all employees. Also, an employer cannot force a person to retire if they become disabled.

Claiming benefits as a result of a work-related disability
Industrial Injuries disablement benefit

You might get Industrial Injuries Disablement Benefit (IIDB) if you're ill or disabled from an accident or disease caused by work while you were on an approved employment training scheme or course. The amount you may get depends on your individual circumstances. Your carer could get Carer's Allowance if you have substantial caring needs.

What you'll get
The level of your disability will affect the amount of benefit you may get. This will be assessed by a 'medical advisor' on a scale of 1 to 100%. Normally you must be assessed as 14% disabled or more to get the benefit.

The amounts outlined below are a guide only.

Assessed level of disablement	Weekly amount
100%	£168.00
90%	£151.20
80%	£134.40
70%	£117.60
60%	£100.80
50%	£84.00
40%	£67.20
30%	£50.40
20%	£33.60

Eligibility
Accidents
You may be able to claim Industrial Injuries Disablement Benefit if:
- o you were employed when the accident or event happened
- o you were on an approved employment training scheme or course when the accident or event happened

o the work accident or event that caused your illness or disability happened in England, Scotland or Wales.

Diseases

You can claim IIDB if you were employed in a job or were on an approved employment training scheme or course that caused your disease. The scheme covers a number of diseases including:
- o asthma
- o chronic bronchitis or emphysema
- o deafness
- o pneumoconiosis (including silicosis and asbestosis)
- o osteoarthritis of the knee in coal miners
- o prescribed disease A11 (previously known as vibration white finger)
- o diffuse mesothelioma and a number of other asbestos-related diseases such as primary carcinoma of the lung

The scheme also covers asbestos related diseases including:
- o pneumoconiosis (asbestosis)
- o diffuse mesothelioma
- o primary carcinoma of the lung with asbestosis
- o primary carcinoma of the lung without asbestosis but where there has been extensive occupational exposure to asbestos in specified occupations
- o unilateral or bilateral diffuse pleural thickening.
- o You can get a full list of illnesses from your regional Industrial Injuries Disablement Benefit centre.

You can't claim Industrial Injuries Disablement Benefit if you were self-employed.

Claiming for Accidents

Print and fill in form BI100A to claim Industrial Injuries Disablement Benefit (IIDB) for accidents.

Diseases

Print and fill in form BI100PD to claim IIDB for diseases. To request a form contact:

Barnsley Industrial Injuries Disablement Benefit centre
Telephone: 0345 758 5433

Send your form to Barrow Industrial Injuries Disablement Benefit Centre if you're claiming under special provisions.

Barrow Benefit Centre
Post Handling Site B
Wolverhampton
WV99 1RX
Telephone: 0345 603 1358
Textphone: 0345 608 8551

For all other claims send your form to Barnsley Industrial Injuries Disablement Benefit centre.

Barnsley IIDB Centre
Mail Handling Site A
Wolverhampton
WV98 1SY
Telephone: 0345 758 5433
Textphone: 0345 608 8551

Other benefits you may be able to get

Constant Attendance Allowance (CAA)
You can claim CAA for accidents where your disability is assessed at 100% and you need daily care and attention. The CAA rate you're paid is based on an assessment of your needs.

Exceptionally Severe Disablement Allowance
You can claim £67.20 paid in addition to the CAA rates, if you're assessed at one of the top two rates of CAA and need permanent, constant care and attention.

Reduced Earnings Allowance (REA)
You may get REA if:

- you can't do your usual job or other work with similar pay because of an accident or disease caused by work
- you have a disability or injury which began before 1 October 1990
- Pneumoconiosis Etc. (Workers' Compensation) Act 1979

Jobcentre Plus may pay you a lump sum if you have one of the following diseases:
- pneumoconiosis
- byssinosis
- diffuse mesothelioma
- bilateral diffuse pleural thickening
- primary carcinoma of the lung when accompanied by asbestosis or bilateral diffuse pleural thickening

To get a payment you must meet all the following conditions:
- your dust-related disease must have been caused by your employment
- you're getting Industrial Injuries Disablement Benefit for one of the listed diseases
- you must claim within 12 months of the decision awarding Industrial Injuries Disablement Benefit
- you can't or haven't taken civil action because your former employer has stopped trading
- you haven't brought a court action or received compensation from an employer in respect of the disease

You may be able to make a claim if you're the dependant of someone who suffered from a dust-related disease but who has died. A dependant claim must be made within 12 months of the death of the sufferer.

Diffuse mesothelioma payment

The scheme covers people whose exposure to asbestos occurred in the United Kingdom and are not entitled to a payment under the Pneumoconiosis etc (Workers' Compensation) Act 1979. For example:

o   they came into contact with asbestos from a relative, eg by washing their clothes
o   their exposure to asbestos was while self-employed

You may be able to claim a one-off lump sum payment if you:

o   are unable to make a claim under the 1979 Pneumoconiosis Act
o   haven't received payment in respect of the disease from an employer, a civil claim or elsewhere
o   aren't entitled to compensation from a Ministry of Defence scheme

Effects on other benefits

You can still get Industrial Injuries Disablement Benefit (IIDB) if you're claiming:

contribution-based Employment and Support Allowance

o   Incapacity Benefit
o   contribution-based Jobseeker's Allowance
o   State Pension

IIDB will affect the following benefits if you or your partner are claiming them:

- o Income Support
- o income-based Jobseeker's Allowance
- o income-related Employment and Support Allowance
- o Pension Credit
- o Housing Benefit
- o Working Tax Credit
- o Universal credit

You should also check to see if Council tax Support has been affected.

****

Chapter 9

Disabled People and Education

It's against the law for a school or other education provider to treat disabled students unfavourably. This includes: 'direct discrimination', eg refusing admission to a student because of disability; 'indirect discrimination', eg only providing application forms in one format that may not be accessible; 'discrimination arising from a disability', eg a disabled pupil is prevented from going outside at break time because it takes too long to get there; 'harassment', eg a teacher shouts at a disabled student for not paying attention when the student's disability stops them from easily concentrating and victimisation, eg suspending a disabled student because they've complained about harassment.

Reasonable adjustments

As with employers, an education provider has a duty to make 'reasonable adjustments' to make sure disabled students are not discriminated against. These changes could include changes to physical features, eg creating a ramp so that students can enter a classroom,providing extra support and aids (like specialist teachers or equipment)

Portage

It is worth at this point mentioning portage, which can benefit your child pre-school. Portage is a home-visiting educational service for pre-school children with additional support needs and their families. Portage Home Visitors are employed by Local Authorities and Charities to support children and families within their local community. The Portage model of learning is characterised by the following attributes:

- regular home visiting;
- supporting the development of play, communication, relationships, and learning for young children within the family;
- supporting the child and family's participation and inclusion in the community in their own right;
- working together with parents within the family, with them taking the leading role in the partnership that is established;
- helping parents to identify what is important to them and their child and plan goals for learning and participation;
- keeping a shared record of the child's progress and other issues raised by the family;
- responding flexibly to the needs of the child and family when providing support;
- You can find out more about Portage by contacting The National Portage Association address at the end of the chapter.

Special Educational Needs (SEN)

All publicly-funded pre-schools, nurseries, state schools and local authorities must try to identify and help assess children with Special Educational Needs. If a child has a statement of special educational needs, they should have a 'transition plan' drawn up in Year 9. This helps to plan what support the child will have after leaving school.

Higher education

All universities and higher education colleges should have a person in charge of disability issues that you can talk to about the support they offer. You can also ask local social services for an assessment to help with your day-to-day living needs.

Special educational needs support
Your child will get SEN support at their school or college. Your child may need an education, health and care (EHC) plan if they need more support than their school provides.

Children under 5
SEN support for children under 5 includes:
- a written progress check when your child is 2 years old
- a child health visitor carrying out a health check for your child if they're aged 2 to 3
- a written assessment in the summer term of your child's first year of primary school
- making reasonable adjustments for disabled children, like providing aids like tactile signs

Nurseries, playgroups and childminders registered with Ofsted follow the Early Years Foundation Stage (EYFS) framework. The framework makes sure that there's support in place for children with SEND.

Talk to a doctor or health adviser if you think your child has SEND but they don't go to a nursery, playgroup or childminder. They'll tell you what support options are available.

Children between 5 and 15
Talk to the teacher or the SEN co-ordinator (SENCO) if you think your child needs:
- a special learning programme
- extra help from a teacher or assistant
- to work in a smaller group
- observation in class or at break

- help taking part in class activities
- extra encouragement in their learning, eg to ask questions or to try something they find difficult
- help communicating with other children
- support with physical or personal care difficulties, eg eating, getting around school safely or using the toilet

Young people aged 16 or over in further education

Contact the college before your child starts further education to make sure that they can meet your child's needs. The college and your local authority will talk to your child about the support they need.

Extra help

An education, health and care (EHC) plan is for children and young people aged up to 25 who need more support than is available through special educational needs support. EHC plans identify educational, health and social needs and set out the additional support to meet those needs.

Requesting an EHC assessment

You can ask your local authority to carry out an assessment if you think your child needs an EHC plan. A young person can request an assessment themselves if they're aged 16 to 25.

A request can also be made by anyone else who thinks an assessment may be necessary, including doctors, health visitors, teachers, parents and family friends. If they decide to carry out an assessment you may be asked for:

- any reports from your child's school, nursery or childminder
- doctors' assessments of your child
- a letter from you about your child's needs

The local authority will tell you within 16 weeks whether an EHC plan is going to be made for your child.

Creating an EHC plan

Your local authority will create a draft EHC plan and send you a copy. You have 15 days to comment, including if you want to ask that your child goes to a specialist needs school or specialist college. Your local authority has 20 weeks from the date of the assessment to give you the final EHC plan.

Disagreeing with a decision

You can challenge your local authority about:

- their decision to not carry out an assessment
- their decision to not create an EHC plan
- the special educational support in the EHC plan
- the school named in the EHC plan

If you can't resolve the problem with your local authority, you can appeal to the Special Educational Needs and Disability (SEND) Tribunal.

Personal budgets

You may be able to get a personal budget for your child if they have an EHC plan or have been told that they need one. It allows you to have a say in how to spend the money on support for your child.

There are 3 ways you can use your personal budget. You can have:

- direct payments made into your account - you buy and manage services yourself
- an arrangement with your local authority or school where they hold the money for you but you still decide how to spend it (sometimes called 'notional arrangements')

- third-party arrangements - you choose someone else to manage the money for you

You can have a combination of all 3 options.

Independent support for children of all ages
Independent supporters can help you and your child through the new SEN assessment process, including:
- replacing a statement of special educational needs with a new EHC plan
- moving a child from a learning difficulty assessment (LDA) to an EHC plan

You can find out how to get local support through:
- Council for Disabled Children
- Information, Advice and Support Service Network
- your local authority website and search for 'Local Offer'

If your child got support before September 2014
Your child will continue to get support until they're moved across to special educational needs (SEN) support or an education, health and care (EHC) plan. Your child should have moved to:

- SEN Support by summer 2015 if they already got help through School Action, School Action Plus, Early Years Action or Early Years Action Plus
- an EHC plan by spring 2018 if they have a statement
- an EHC plan by September 2016 if they have an LDA

Early Years Action and School Action
This support is either a different way of teaching certain things, or some help from an extra adult.

Early Years Action Plus and School Action Plus
This is extra help from an external specialist, eg a speech therapist.

Assessments
An assessment of special educational needs involves experts and people involved in your child's education. They ask about your child's needs and what should be done to meet them.

Statement
A statement of special education needs describes your child's needs and how they should be met, including what school they should go to.

Further education
If your child has a statement of special educational needs, they'll have a 'transition plan' drawn up in Year 9. This helps to plan for their future after leaving school.

Disabled people and financing studies
Financial support for all students comes in the form of tuition fee loans, means tested loans for living expenses and also a range of supplementary grants and loans depending on individual circumstances. Entitlement to student support depends on where you are living and where you intend to study. For details of loan entitlement and rates also Bursaries, you should contact:

Student finance England if you reside in England
www.gov.uk/student-finance
Northern Ireland Student finance NI 0300 100 0077
www.studentfinanceni.co.uk
Scotland Student Awards Agency for Scotland www.saas.gov.uk
Wales Student Finance Wales 0300 400 4050
www.studentfianncewales.co.uk

For details of loans and bursaries plus other sources of finance, you should contact the student support officer responsible for advice at the educational institution that you are to attend.

Students and means tested benefits

If you are a disabled student and want more information on benefits entitlement and how being a student in higher education affects benefits then you should contact the Disability Advisor at your local Jobcentre Plus. Essentially, benefit entitlement will depend very much on your individual circumstances and what type of education you are undertaking.

*****

Chapter 10

Disabled People and Housing Rights

This chapter covers the rights of disabled people and occupation of a property. In the main, it deals with the responsibilities of private and social landlords and with the responsibilities of tenants. We also discuss accessing finance to purchase a property and the provision of disabled facilities grants to help the process of living in a property that much easier.

The law generally relating to tenants rights covers all people but there are also separate rights protecting those with disabilities. This chapter covers Disabled Housing in England. For housing rights and disabled in Wales, Scotland and Northern Ireland go to:

https://scotland.shelter.org.uk (Scotland)

https://www.housingadviceni.org/accessible-housing (Ireland)

https://sheltercymru.org.uk (Wales)

Introduction

In most parts of the country now, there are relatively few social properties available, and increasing numbers of people are renting from private landlords, which h brings with it different problems, which we cover below. Renting from a private landlord is different to renting from a social housing provider in several ways: – There are lots of homes available to rent privately (depending where you live of course). That gives you a good chance of finding a home where you want to live, e.g. near to your family and friends, schools, work, or health facilities. In addition, you will usually be able to find a property more quickly: this is very helpful if you need to move to a new area to start a course or a job, or you need a place temporarily while you wait for social housing or save up to buy a property. If you are homeless, the council may well place you in private rented property – at least temporarily, or even permanently (although this will be governed by supply and demand in an area..

In the private sector you should be aware that: – The rent is likely to be higher than in the social rented sector. – If you are entitled to either Housing Benefit or the housing element of Universal Credit, you can use this to pay your rent; however, it may not   cover the full cost. It can be more difficult (but may be possible) to make changes to a private rented property so that it meets your needs. There is less 'security of tenure' – in other words, it is easier for your landlord to ask you to move out, even if you have been a good tenant.

Private renting in England
Some private landlords use a 'letting agency' to manage their properties. They act as a 'go-between': sometimes just to find tenants and set the tenancy up; sometimes to provide ongoing management, in which case they will be your first port of call if there are any problems with the property after you have moved in. Sometimes the letting agency is 'social', i.e. not-for-profit. Some housing associations run a social letting agency and may manage properties on behalf of private landlords.

What is 'affordable housing' or 'intermediate market rent'?
Increasing numbers of (especially new-build) housing association properties are let as 'affordable' rather than 'social' housing. The rent is referred to as 'affordable', but it is set at a higher level than would normally be charged for social housing. The landlord can charge up to 80% of what it would cost if you were renting the property privately (inclusive of any service charge that may be

payable). The extra money housing associations make from this goes towards building new social housing.

Some of this housing is designated for people who are not on benefits but cannot afford to buy a property. The idea is that they can save the money they would have spent renting privately for a deposit to buy a property, usually through the Help to Buy scheme. This is particularly common in areas where houses are very expensive. Other social landlords offer private rented properties (i.e. with assured shorthold tenancies) at full market rent. Some have special packages for 'key workers' (people who provide an essential service in the public sector, such as those employed in the NHS). You can check whether housing association schemes are members of The National Approved Letting Scheme (NALS).

Can you rent specialist housing for older people privately?
Retirement living properties, which usually have above-average accessibility and may benefit from on-site support and care, are an option for disabled people aged 55 and over. Normally you would apply via your council to either rent (social rent) or buy a leasehold property. However, there is also an emerging private rent market for these properties, either from individuals who own them, or from providers themselves.

Despite the number of properties available to rent at any time, it can be challenging to find somewhere that meets your access requirements – or even to find out whether a property does or does not meet your access requirements. This is especially true if you need somewhere that is fully wheelchair-accessible. Many private landlords and letting agencies advertise available properties online, using the rental pages of websites such as Zoopla and Rightmove. However, these websites don't currently allow you to search for accessible properties or particular access features. Rightmove can filter searches for bungalows, but these may or may not be fully accessible.

It can be a good idea to contact letting agencies that operate in the area you want to live and explain your access requirements to them. You could search for an Association of Residential Lettings Agents (ARLA) Propertymark Protected letting agent. They may be able to identify potential properties for you and let you know as soon as they become available – though you may need to build this relationship and check in with them regularly. You should also be aware that letting agencies' loyalties ultimately lie with the landlord, so do not expect them to give you completely impartial advice.

Lettings agents must by law make their application processes (e.g. any forms you need to complete) accessible to you.

There are also some companies who specialise in finding accessible properties –again, check that they are registered with ARLA. In some areas, there are 'social' (not for profit) lettings agencies and the criteria for using these agencies varies. For example, sometimes you need to be homeless and referred by the council –but it is worth finding out. Your council will be able to advise.

You should also speak to the housing options team at your council if you have not already done so. If you are at risk of homelessness or your current property is so unsuitable for your needs that you could be described as effectively homeless, they should help you consider your housing options in both the social and private rented sector. They may be able to refer you to a social letting agency or give you a list of private letting agencies operating in your area. Even if your housing needs are not so urgent, they may still be able to give you some pointers on trying to find an adapted or accessible property locally, and/or accessing funding locally to help meet the cost of adaptations. Arrange to view any properties that sound promising to see if they actually work for you.

The lettings process
Pre-tenancy checks

Before you can rent a property, you will need to show your passport or another document that demonstrates you have a right to rent in the UK. The landlord or letting agency want to be sure you will be a good tenant. There are various ways of doing this, and some are more flexible than others: – You may be asked for references from current or previous landlords, employers, or someone else who can vouch that you will be a good tenant. – You will probably be asked for evidence that you can afford the rent, e.g. benefit letters, payslips/work contracts, bank statements (make sure you hide the account number). – They will usually want to run a credit check. – Alternatively, you may be able to use a 'guarantor' – this is someone who signs to say they are willing to pay the rent if you do not, and is usually a family member who will need to meet certain financial criteria themselves. You can find more detailed advice on the Citizens Advice website.

Payments at the start of the tenancy

You will generally need to pay your rent monthly and in advance. This means you will need to pay a month's rent upfront. At the start of the tenancy, you will also often need to pay the landlord a deposit. This is to protect them against the risk of you damaging the property and/or leaving without paying the rent. The landlord must put this in one of three government-backed 'tenancy deposit schemes' within 30 days. These schemes will make sure you get all your deposit back at the end of the tenancy, provided you keep to your side of the tenancy agreement.

It is possible that you will be able to get help with the payments at the start of a tenancy, through a rent deposit, bond and guarantee scheme run by a council, housing association or charity. Most of these are given to people who are homeless and/or 'vulnerable', so you will need to be in urgent housing need. You could check Crisis's Help to Rent database to see if there are any schemes in your area, though you will need to check with the local scheme to find out if you are eligible.

How to rent guide

It is now law for your landlord (or letting agent) to hand you a copy of the How to rent guide at the start of the tenancy. This outlines what you and your landlord should expect from each other. It contains important information, such as: – questions to ask once you have found a property – how to navigate the ending of your tenancy – what to do if things go wrong.

My rights and responsibilities as a tenant
The tenancy

The tenancy is the contract between you ('the tenant') and the person who owns the property ('the landlord'), which allows you to live in it. The tenancy sets out the rights and responsibilities of both the tenant and the landlord. Tenants have rights, but also have responsibilities: most notably, to pay your rent on time and to keep the property in a reasonable condition. The tenancy should state the amount of rent due, when it should be paid and how long the contract lasts.

Most private tenants have an 'assured shorthold tenancy'. Since housing law has changed over time, if your tenancy started before February 1997, you should check what kind of tenancy you have. It should say on the tenancy document you have from your landlord. You may have an assured or protected tenancy, in which case you have slightly different rights. See the Citizens Advice website for more details on this. The UK Government has produced a model tenancy agreement. Landlords don't have to use it but it is free to use, so you could suggest this (or compare and check against the tenancy agreement you are issued with). Your tenancy may also include an 'inventory' – this lists any furniture and fittings that are provided with the property and the condition they are in at the start of the tenancy. You should agree this carefully at the outset with the landlord/letting agency. If you ask your landlord to provide the tenancy document in a version that is accessible to you (e.g. braille, audio, large print, easy read, another language) they must (under the Equality Act 2010) do so. Everyone should have the opportunity to ask questions about their tenancy at sign-up, whatever their access and communication needs.

Making adaptations to a property

If you are finding it difficult to access basic facilities in your home or feel unsafe getting around your property, you may benefit from a home adaptation. Aids and adaptations are not only for people with reduced mobility; they may also help people with sensory impairments, dementia or mental health conditions. They could range from a small piece of equipment or technology right through to a major structural change, with the aim of improving your independence, confidence and privacy. If you live in a block of flats with some communal facilities, your landlord can make 'reasonable adjustments' to improve access to and within communal areas.

If equipment or an adaptation costs less than £1,000, your council (or in some cases the NHS) should provide this for free. You will need to get the permission of your landlord to make a change to your property, but, under the Equality Act 2010, they cannot refuse unless they have 'reasonable grounds' for doing so. Examples of things to look at to decide whether your landlord has a good reason for refusing an adaptation include: > the type and length of the letting > your ability to pay for the improvement > how easy it is to make the adaptations (and how easy it would be to undo them), and > the extent of any disruption and effect on other occupiers. – If the adaptation costs more than £1,000, you will need to apply for a Disabled Facilities Grant (DFG) from your local housing authority. DFGs are generally means-tested but the council cannot refuse this solely because you are a private rented tenant, if you and your landlord are willing to confirm that you plan to stay in the property for the next five years. This is confirmed by the tenant and owner submitting a 'tenant's certificate' and an 'owner's certificate' respectively.

There are exceptions where the landlord can refuse to make the improvements, particularly if you are renting a room in a shared house, for example if: – the property you are renting has been the main home of the landlord – you share facilities such as the kitchen, bathroom or living room (the exception does not apply when you only share access to the property or storage areas) – the landlord or landlord's family member lives in the property, or – the property is not large enough to accommodate more than six lodgers or two separate households. At the moment, the Equality Act 2010 does not require the landlord to make structural changes to your property, or the 'common parts' of a block of flats.

Dealing with problems in your tenancy
Problems with heating, appliances and repairs

Your landlord has legal obligations to ensure that their property is safe for you to live in. If your health is negatively affected by the condition of the property, you may be within your rights to demand repairs to rectify the problem. Landlords are legally responsible for ensuring that: – the building's structure is sound, including external roofs, walls, windows and doors. – internal sanitation and plumbing is fully functional and safe, and that heating and hot water is properly maintained. – chimneys and other means of ventilation are safe and in good working order. – gas appliances are safely installed and maintained by a Gas Safe registered engineer, who must provide an annual gas safety check on appliances and flues: you should be given a copy of the gas safety record within 28 days of the check, all electrical goods and mains are safe, including fixtures and any equipment they supply with the property, fire safety regulations are followed, including installing smoke alarms, fire safe furniture and fittings, and providing access to escape routes: these need to be accessible to you. If you live in a House in Multiple Occupation (HMO),2 large properties are required to have a fire alarm system and extinguishers installed. HMOs must have a HMO Licence under UK law. To check that a HMO Licence is in place, you can contact your council. Failure of the landlord to comply may lead to their prosecution and/or imprisonment. If you think your landlord is failing on any of the above, you should complain to them (larger landlords or letting agencies should have a formal complaints procedure). Putting complaints in writing/email and keeping a copy can be helpful should you end up taking legal action.

Eviction by your landlord

There are special rules regarding your right to stay in the property and your landlord's power to make you leave. You may face eviction if you do not pay your full rent or if you break the terms of your tenancy agreement. However, the landlord must still apply to the court and follow correct procedure before you are evicted, issuing a 'Section 8 Notice' against you. A 'Section 8 Notice' can be used where you have breached your tenancy agreement during the fixed period of your tenancy (the amount of time that your tenancy is for, which will be written in your tenancy agreement). There are different grounds that the landlord can rely on to evict you. Some of these grounds are mandatory – if they are proved, the court must grant an order evicting you – and some are discretionary – the court may or may not order eviction. Most commonly, landlords evict people using a 'Section 21 Notice': this is the form they use to start eviction proceedings in cases where the fixed period of your tenancy has come to an end. If you are still in the fixed period of your tenancy, proceedings cannot be issued until this fixed period expires, though the 'Section 21 Notice' may be sent to you before that date. This is usually used when landlords want to sell, refurbish or use the property differently. They do not have to give any reason for this, but they do need to follow a set of rules for this to be valid.

Landlords are prevented from serving a 'Section 21 Notice' if you have complained about your property needing repair and this work has not been done before the 'Section 21 Notice' is sent to you. More information is available on Shelter's website. Call the police immediately if you are being illegally evicted and threatened with violence.

If you are facing eviction, you should contact your council's housing options team and/or seek assistance from Shelter. You should do this at the soonest opportunity; if you leave before you have to, your council may decide you have made yourself 'intentionally homeless'. If you have asked your landlord to make repairs to your property, which they refuse to complete, and they try to evict you as a result, they are in breach of their obligations to you as its tenant. However, the degree to which you can challenge a 'retaliatory eviction' depends on when your tenancy began. More detail, as well as information that will help you decide what type of tenancy you have, is available on the Citizens Advice website.

Getting your deposit back when you move out
You should get your deposit back when you move out, but the landlord can make 'reasonable' deductions from this to cover unpaid rent, damage to the property, missing items (listed in the inventory) and/or cleaning costs. If you think your landlord is being unreasonable or they are refusing to give the deposit back, there are steps you can take. For example, the deposit protection scheme has a free Dispute Resolution Service. Shelter sets out the steps you should take in some detail on their website.

Making complaints
Many complaints can be solved by discussing the issue with your landlord in the first instance. If this fails, there are a number of ways you can make a formal complaint. Check if your landlord or letting agency has a complaints procedure. Make complaints by email or in writing (keeping a copy). Where disputes are unresolved, you could complain to a 'designated person', which might be your MP or local councillor, or contact your council for

further advice. Your council's private sector licensing or enforcement team or, in the case of problems like pests, damp and leaks, their environmental health team may be able to help. Citizens Advice offer further advice on their website on complaining about your landlord.

Information about private renting
Shelter offers many online resources, including: – Housing advice – Contact a housing advisor. Citizens Advice also provides advice and guidance. The Tenants' Voice is the biggest tenant community in the UK, and has a website full of information about renting and getting advice related to your renting problems.

Finding an advocate
An advocate can help you express your views and stand up for your rights. Your council may fund an advocacy service in your area, so check with them. If you have a mental health condition, see Mind's website. If you have a cognitive impairment,

Citizens Advice has a dedicated webpage on taking action on discrimination in housing. If you think you have experienced discrimination, you can get help and advice from the Equality Advisory and Support Service.

Legal help
Legal aid (to help pay for legal presentation in civil cases) is not as readily available as it used to be. However, there are still particular circumstances in which you might be eligible to receive it, and there are some remaining sources of free legal advice. See Shelter's website. If you are at risk of harm

If you are at risk of harm, you must seek advice as soon as possible from your council's housing options team. You can find the website of your local council. It may also a good idea to get independent advice from Shelter or Citizens Advice. Other sources of support

Local or impairment-specific disability charities may be able to offer support. You could contact your local councillor or MP You can find out who they are by entering your postcode on the UK Government website or UK Parliament website. The Samaritans can provide emotional support and should be able to suggest sources of practical help and advocacy in your area. You don't need to be suicidal.

Social Housing
What is 'social housing'?
'Social housing' is owned by a housing association (also known as a 'Registered Provider'), a council (also known as a local authority) or sometimes by a housing cooperative or charity. It is intended for people on low incomes and is usually rented to them; though some housing associations also offer shared ownership (part-rent, part-buy) properties. Unlike private landlords, housing associations are not profit-making; they must use any surplus money they make to maintain existing homes and build new ones. 'Social' or 'affordable'?

Affordable rent is a type of social housing provided in England by social housing landlords. The rent is called 'affordable', but it is a higher rent than would normally be charged for social housing. The landlord can charge up to 80% of what it would cost if you were renting the property privately. This is in contrast to 'social rent', for which guideline target rents are set by the national rent regime.

Who can apply for social housing?
If you are over the age of 16 you can apply for social housing while in a variety of situations: if you are homeless; if you already have a social or privately rented property; if you own your own home but are looking to sell; or if you are staying with family and friends. Social housing can offer many benefits over and above the private rented sector, including cheaper rents and more 'security of tenure'. This means that a social landlord cannot make you leave

the property as easily as a private landlord can, and only if you have failed to meet your responsibilities as a tenant, which should be set out clearly at the start of your tenancy. It is also generally easier to have adaptations made to a social rented than a private rented property Each person's needs and circumstances are different, and you will need to decide what is right for you, depending on what is available in the area(s) in which you want to live. Some social housing may be suitable for you; some may not.

How to get a (new) property
In many areas, most − if not all − housing associations and any remaining council properties are let through a 'Common Housing Register'. This is a single point of access for social rented properties, so you do not have to approach each provider separately. You can find out about how this works in your area online or in person through your council's housing options team or advice centre. You can enter a postcode to find the local authority covering your area and go to their website.

If you live in an area covered by a county council, it will be your local district council that you need to approach for housing. You should check whether there are any social housing providers that are not part of the Common Housing Register: if you want to apply to them, you might need to complete a separate housing application.

Councils must allow homeless people, disabled people or those with health or welfare needs to join the register. Councils may require people to have a strong 'local connection'. You need to fill in a form to apply to join the Common Housing Register − sometimes this is online, sometimes in person, or often you can choose. If you need help to fill in the form, due to access or communication needs, the council should provide this. Libraries can also often offer assistance and online access. You must make sure the information on your application is kept up to date if there are changes to your household or current housing circumstances, or if a medical condition worsens, for example.

Making the case for your housing needs

First, find out exactly how decisions about who gets social housing are made in the area where you want to live. You need to either search online or ask the council for its allocation policy or scheme. This should set out clearly the rules and the method for ranking the urgency of people's need for (re-)housing.– Many areas only accept or prioritise people with a 'local connection' or 'residential requirement'. If you are not already living in the area where you are applying to live, you may need to demonstrate a connection to it, e.g. close family living there, or a job offer. If you are trying to move to a different local authority area because you will have more support from family living there, you should explain this and make the point that this move should reduce your (current and/or future) need for care and support from social services. Sometimes people applying for housing are given a number of 'points' (the more points, the higher priority they are considered to be); sometimes they are put in 'bands' (e.g. high/medium/low, or 'eligible' and 'urgent'). The allocation scheme should explain which bands or points apply to different sorts of housing circumstances in your area.

If your disability or medical condition is the primary reason for moving, you will need to build a strong case, e.g. by spelling out exactly why your current housing circumstances are causing 'significant hardship' or increasing the risk of an 'emergency' (or whatever language the scheme uses). Think about how your current housing is affecting your physical and mental health, and your independence. Highlight any risks that result from living there, e.g. of falls or other accidents.

If you are at risk of harm or of becoming homeless, you must seek advice as soon as possible from your council's housing options team. It is also a good idea to get independent advice from Shelter or Citizens Advice. Local or impairment-specific disability charities may also be able to offer advocacy and support. Women's Aid and Refuge run a 24-hour freephone advice line for female and male victims of domestic violence (0808 2000 247). If you do not feel you are receiving the response you need, you could also contact your local councillor or MP, or Samaritans who can provide emotional support and should also be able to suggest sources of practical help and advocacy in your area. If you disagree with the decision regarding the priority you have been given

The council will give you a deadline for requesting a review – this is usually 21 days after you have received the decision. Put your request in writing: provide any new medical or supporting information to help your case (an occupational therapist might be well-placed to provide this). Include any information that shows the council has made a mistake. Again, try to get advice from Citizens' Advice, Shelter or a local advice provider.

Finding a suitable property
You need to find out how properties are 'allocated' or matched to people in your area. This should be included in the allocation scheme, or you can find out from your council's website, at a library, from individual housing associations, from Citizens Advice or your council's advice centre. Many, but not all, councils now operate a 'choice-based lettings' system. In other areas, councils make 'direct offers' of housing. Even in areas where there is a choice-based lettings system, it is likely that there will be some direct offers made by the council in very specific circumstances, or perhaps by individual housing associations which are not part of the Common Housing Register. In some council areas, all adapted properties are allocated outside of the choice-based lettings system. Choice-based lettings systems

In a choice-based lettings system, the available properties are advertised and you say which you are interested in by 'bidding'.

Once you've been accepted onto the waiting list, you should follow these basic steps:

1. Find a property: check in local papers, on council websites, in council offices or in local libraries.

2. Check you can apply for it: some properties are only suitable for single people, families or people with certain access requirements. Note that disabled people must not be restricted to bidding only for accessible homes as this would breach the duty to promote disability equality.

3. Find out whether the property will meet your access requirements and/or whether it could be adapted. Some councils will allocate properties that have already been significantly adapted outside of the choice-based lettings system, so you need to check the policy in your area (see Direct offers). The level of detail supplied on choice-based lettings adverts regarding the layout, size, accessibility and exact location of properties varies considerably.

Think carefully about what you need as an absolute minimum to stay physically and mentally well, what you might be able to adapt or live with, and what would be nice to have, but not essential. If you need more information about a property's suitability in order to decide whether or not to bid for it, contact the council's housing department and ask them. Explain that you need to understand whether it will be accessible to you as a disabled person. If you are told that this service is not available, you could argue that this would be a reasonable adjustment under the Equality Act 2010.

4. Apply: this is known as 'bidding', but it doesn't involve money. You can usually bid online, by phone or by text. Get the social housing provider's decision on whether or not you will be offered that property. The decision will also tell you how many other people bid for this property, which bands they were in and how

many points they had. This can give you an indication of your chances of success.

Direct offers

Some areas do not have a choice-based lettings system, but instead will make a direct offer when you are at the top of the list, or if an adapted property that meets your needs becomes available. Even in areas that operate a choice-based lettings system, if an individual or household needs a very specific property (e.g. in terms of size or layout) it may be that a direct offer can be made outside of the system. You need to contact your housing office/ council to ask if you might be eligible and what the implications of this might be, for example, there will almost certainly only be one direct offer made to you if a 'suitable' property is found, so you need to be prepared to compromise on some aspects, such as the exact location of the property. Again, it can be a good idea to list your preferences in order and think about which you can and cannot compromise on.

What if the application system is not accessible to me?

Under the Equality Act 2010, councils and housing associations have a duty to make 'reasonable adjustments' so you can access the housing application process. This might, for example, involve providing: – the application form in alternative formats (e.g. braille, large print, coloured paper, audio) – help to complete the housing application form – help to understand how the system works, and – advice and support on bidding for properties. If you need help viewing properties in order to check whether they will meet your access requirements, you should ask the council if they can help. If they are not able to provide this directly, you may be able to get this support from a local disability charity, voluntary sector organisation or from your occupational therapist.

*

What if I don't agree that the offer made to me is 'suitable'?

If a direct offer is made to you but it does not meet your needs, you can appeal against the decision by making a complaint, requesting a review, or – if this is unsuccessful – taking this to the Housing Ombudsman or even judicial review (a court challenge against the legality of a decision made by a public body – it should be noted that this is a costly process).

If you feel that a property you have been offered does not meet your needs (arising from your medical condition or impairment) then you need to put together as much specific evidence as you can of why this is. This might be: – about your ability to get in, out of and around the property independently. – that the property meets your needs now but is unlikely to do so within the next few years. – that the location of the property means you will be unable to move around safely in the immediate vicinity (e.g. because the ground is very uneven or hilly, or because you are visually impaired and the property is on a busy road with no accessible crossing). – because of reasons linked to your mental health as well as your physical safety and independence.– if living here is likely to increase your need for social care – you should spell this out and enlist the support of your social worker. – if it is likely to increase the risk of you falling or having an accident – an occupational therapist or GP might be able to write you a letter or support you. Due to the lack of accessible affordable housing, some disabled people find themselves being offered (or even, in the case of one of our focus group participants, being 'bullied into accepting') older people's supported housing, even though they are much younger than the average person in this type of housing.

Supported properties vary enormously in layout (for example, some have their own front door off the street), quality, and diversity of other residents, so – in areas of high demand – it is always worth visiting them to get a feel for the place, rather than ruling it out automatically. You should not feel pressured into accepting a property that you believe will have a negative impact on your psychological and social identity, even if it is physically accessible.

Finding an adapted or accessible property
Mutual exchange

If you are an existing social tenant, you can look for a suitable adapted/ accessible property using HomeSwapper or Ukhomeswap. These schemes allow different tenants of social landlords to swap properties so that both parties' housing needs are met, though you need to be careful that the exchanger has presented the accessibility of the property accurately. You can access either of the websites yourself to find out more, to enrol and to search for properties. However, disabled house-seekers may find it easier to get help from their housing officer to access these schemes: the officer should explore the available housing options with you.

There are a small number of housing associations which specialise in providing accessible properties, such as Habinteg and Ability Housing. Supported housing for older people

If you are an 'older' adult, there may be social rented properties specifically for older people available in your area. The lower age limit for these properties varies, but is often 55 for disabled people and those who have support needs and/or long-term health conditions. The quality and accessibility of the accommodation, availability of support and other services, and mix of people in the properties, can vary enormously in these schemes. Schemes may be described as 'sheltered housing', 'retirement/independent living', 'extra care' or 'housing with care' (where there is an onsite team, should you need personal care). The types of housing for older people are complex and need to be fully explored in order to meet individual needs. Information and guidance on the different housing models is available on the Age UK website. HousingCare provides a UK-wide searchable database of older people's supported housing, care homes and services, as well as services that support people staying in their own homes.

First Stop provides advice on older people's housing, care and support, including a number of factsheets and an email/livechat helpline. Email: info@firststopcareadvice.org.

Your rights as a tenant

The tenancy is the legal agreement between you ('the tenant') and the owner of the property (in this case, the housing association, council, co-operative or charity) ('the landlord'), which allows you to live in the property. The tenancy agreement sets out the rights and responsibilities of both tenant and landlord. We focus here on your rights, but you also have responsibilities, e.g. to pay your rent on time, to keep the property in a reasonable condition, and not to get in the way of your neighbours' rights to enjoy their homes. Housing law has changed over time. As a result, social tenants have different types of tenancies, with some variations.

Many social landlords will issue an 'assured shorthold' (or 'starter' or 'introductory') tenancy to a new tenant for the first 12-18 months, to make sure they are reliable. If this period passes smoothly, they will offer you an 'assured' tenancy or a 'secure tenancy' (either on a fixed-term basis, for example for two years, or indefinitely), in which your right to remain in the property is more secure. If you have been in your property a long time (e.g. since before 1989) you will usually have a 'secure' tenancy. It is important to check the type of tenancy you have: before the start of a new social tenancy, the landlord will send you a written tenancy agreement to sign. The core rights of each of these tenancies include the right to: – stay in the accommodation as long as you keep to the terms of the tenancy agreement with your landlord – have the accommodation kept in a reasonable state of repair, and – enforce your rights, without being evicted for doing so. You also have the right not to be treated unfairly by your landlord because of your disability, gender identity, pregnancy and maternity, race, religion or belief, sex or sexual orientation.

Your rights as a disabled person

If you are disabled (the legal definition of 'disabled' is available on the UK Government website). Your social landlord has a duty under the Equality Act 2010 to make 'reasonable adjustments' or provide 'auxiliary aids and services' so that you can rent and live in a property. This might, for example, include: − providing written agreements in a way that is accessible to you, such as large print, braille, audio, easy read, or in a language other than English. − making changes so you can use any facilities and benefits that come with the property in the same way as a non-disabled tenant, e.g. a wider parking space, or a ramp to access the common garden, and − holding the tenant panel meetings in a room with a hearing loop fitted so you can attend and participate. This does not necessarily mean that the landlord is required to make structural changes to your property

Your landlord only has a duty to make them if they are 'reasonable' − this will depend on: the length and type of tenancy you have; the cost of the adjustment (and the landlord's financial circumstances), and how effective the adjustment is likely to be. Your social landlord also has a duty under the Equality Act 2010 to change a policy or practice (including the term of a tenancy agreement) if it disadvantages you because you are disabled.

ADAPTING A HOME

What is a 'home adaptation'?

If you are finding it difficult to access basic facilities in your home or feel unsafe getting around your property, you may benefit from a home adaptation. Aids and adaptations aren't only for people with reduced mobility; they may also help people with sensory impairments, dementia or even mental health conditions. They could range from a small piece of equipment or technology right through to a major structural change, with the aim of improving your independence, confidence and privacy. Adaptations aren't just about physical access − they might, for example, include building a separate room for a child with autism who is not able to share with a sibling, or changing lighting and acoustics to reduce stress for a person living with dementia. For an adaptation to work, you need to make sure you have found the right solution for your individual needs and the property you live in.

It is important to understand the differences between 'equipment', 'minor adaptations' and 'major adaptations', as the process for accessing them and rules around funding differ for each.

Equipment

'Equipment' is generally portable and can be loaned for a period of time or taken by a person to another property. Examples might include: − a portable wheelchair ramp or raised toilet seat − adapted kitchen utensils and equipment − a hearing aid. Funding and access Equipment is usually provided free of charge (or on some occasions with a small deposit, e.g. £20) if you are assessed as needing it by: − a trusted assessor (who might be an occupational therapist − or social worker) working for the local authority, or − a health professional (GP, hospital clinic, district nurse, community physiotherapist).

Minor adaptations

'Minor adaptions' are changes that are made to the home and typically cost up to £1,000. Examples might include: − a short ramp and/or some grab rails − a door-release intercom system − changes to lighting and paintwork for a person with dementia and/or low vision. Minor adaptations can be approved and funded by your local authority, following an occupational therapy assessment, as part of a care assessment by adult social care services.

Major adaptations

'Major adaptations' typically cost over £1,000 and require substantial or structural works to your home. Examples might include: – the installation of a wet floor shower – ramped access that requires the widening of external doorways – replacing kitchen units with adjustable worktops – building an extension on to the property and/or a ground floor bathroom.

Funding and access

Disabled Facilities Grants can help cover the costs of major adaptations, whether you own your property or rent. The Grant is often means-tested based on your income, your partner's income (if applicable) and your savings, so you may well need to pay towards the cost of the work. The Grant is not means-tested if you are applying on behalf of a child under 18. Some local authorities have abandoned means-testing altogether. To start the process, you need to request an assessment for your social care team. Your local or district council is responsible for administering the Grant, which can provide up to £30,000 of funding. You can apply for funding to help with the costs of home adaptations whether you own your home or rent it from either a social or private landlord.

If you rent from a housing association or you are a council tenant, you should find out first from them how to go about applying for a major adaptation. Some may direct you to the council to apply for a Disabled Facilities Grant for major adaptations, but almost all will want to arrange for and oversee the works to your home.

What is 'occupational therapy'?

Occupational therapy, often referred to as OT, is a healthcare profession that focuses on developing, recovering, or maintaining the daily living and working skills of people with physical, mental, or cognitive impairments. It is a good idea to start by speaking to an occupational therapist when you are thinking about equipment or adaptations. Occupational therapy services are available free of charge from the NHS or social services – if you do not already have an occupational therapist, the best thing to do is contact your council's adult social care team, or you could ask your GP to make a referral. You also have the option to use an independent occupational therapist: they will charge a fee, but they usually don't have waiting lists and can offer services that the state does not fund. You can find a private occupational therapist by searching on the Royal College of Occupational Therapists website.

In England, under the Care Act 2014, you are entitled to a Needs Assessment by your council's adult social care team. This should explore how home adaptations might improve your ability to carry out everyday tasks at home.

You may find that there is a long wait for an occupational therapist or a social work assessment. However, once they have assessed you as needing a piece of equipment, this should be provided by the local community equipment store (usually joint funded by health and social services).

The Independent Living Buyers' Guide is a good place to research possible solutions that might work for you. As the title suggests, it is geared more towards people who are willing and able to buy their own equipment, so not all items will be available free through the NHS or your council. There are lots of ways in which technology can be used to promote independent living

Disabled people and buying a home
If you want to apply for a mortgage, either to buy a new property or re-mortgage an existing one, it is important to make sure you are well prepared and seek professional advice.

Getting a mortgage if you're in receipt of sickness benefits or disability benefits
If your income is either partially or mainly made up of benefits, this shouldn't stop you from getting a mortgage. Some lenders are more likely than others to accept disability benefits as income when doing their affordability checks.

Benefit related income that may be considered by potential lending partners:

Employment Support Allowance – 100% of this benefit can be used when assessing what a potential home buyer can afford. This can also be done where the applicant has no employment income.

Disability Living Allowance - 100% of this benefit can be used when assessing what a potential home buyer can afford. This can also be done where the applicant has no employment income.

Personal Independent Payment – 100% of this benefit can be used when assessing what a potential homebuyer can afford. This can also be done where the applicant has no employment income.

Carers Allowance – 100%of this benefit can be used when assessing what a potential home buyer can afford. This can also be done where the applicant has no employment income.

Child Benefit - 100% of this benefit can be used when assessing what a potential home buyer can afford. This can also be done where the applicant has no employment income.

Child and Working Tax Credits - 100% of this benefit can be used when assessing what a potential home buyer can afford. This can also be done where the applicant has no employment income.

Part time income - 100%of this benefit can be used when assessing what a potential home buyer can afford. This can also be done where the applicant has no employment income.

Income Support - 100% of this benefit can be used when assessing what a potential home buyer can afford. This can also be done where the applicant has no employed income. To take the benefit into consideration the applicant must be in receipt of either Disability Living Allowance or Personal Independent Payment.

Help with mortgage interest payments

If you're claiming a benefit such as income-related Employment and Support Allowance or Income Support you might be able to claim help with your mortgage interest payments. This is called

Support for Mortgage Interest. (SMI). If you qualify for SMI you'll get help paying the interest (but not the capital repayments) on up to £200,000 of your mortgage. You can claim this support even if you are in receipt of benefits when you apply for your mortgage. However, please note that not all lenders will count Support for Mortgage Interest as income when deciding whether or not to lend to you.

The Department for Work and Pensions (DWP) can reduce the amount of support you get if it deems your home is too big or is located in an area that is too expensive. If this happens to you, you should explain to the DWP why you need a larger home (for example, you have a live-in carer or need to keep lots of bulky equipment at home),or need to live in a particular area (for example, you have to be near family or a particular hospital);

SMI will only repay the interest on the loan, it will not repay the capital nor will it repay, for example, the insurance premium element in an endowment mortgage. For this reason the approach most commonly adopted is to raise an interest only mortgage. Find out more about Support for Mortgage Interest on the Gov.uk website

Solicitors
You will have to pay the costs involved such as valuation and legal fees, estate agents fees, advertising, disconnection charges and removal costs.

Adaptations
Some people will require some alteration or adaptation to the property. Read above for information on DFG's.

Before you buy your home and move in, it is important that you make sure the help and support you need is already in place. You can discuss this with Adult Social Care.

Your legal rights

If you can afford a mortgage, banks and other lenders are not allowed to reject your application just because you are disabled. Equally, lenders cannot insist that you pay a larger deposit or make larger monthly repayments than non-disabled customers.

****

Chapter 11

Disabled People and Travel

The Equality Act 2010

As we have seen, the Equality Act 2010 is the main Act covering the rights of disabled people. This is the Act that affects people and Transport.

If you're disabled or have reduced mobility you have certain rights under the Equality Act 2010 and also European Union law when you're travelling by air. If you are travelling outside the European Union, you should find out what help will be available from the airline and the airport where you're travelling.

You don't have to be permanently disabled to get help when you're travelling. For example, you may have reduced mobility because you find it difficult to get about because of your age or a short-term injury or illness.

Bus companies have to make sure that disabled people can get on and off buses in safety and without unreasonable difficulty. They should also make sure that you can travel in safety and reasonable comfort.

Ease of use of public transport

Buses or coaches may need to meet the Public Service Vehicle Accessibility Regulations 2000 allowing access to the vehicle for disabled passengers. In the main, vehicles must meet the regulations if they carry more than 22 passengers and were bought into service from 2000 onwards. Buses and coaches covered by the regulations must have:

o   space for a standard wheelchair

- o a boarding device to enable wheelchair users to get on and off
- o a minimum number of priority seats for disabled passengers
- o handrails to assist disabled people
- o colour contrasting of handrails and steps to help partially sighted people
- o easy to use bell pushes
- o equipment to display the route and destination.

Older buses have to be made accessible to wheelchair users or fitted with accessibility facilities between 2015 and 2020. The speed at which older buses are being replaced by wheelchair user friendly vehicles varies from area to area.

As a wheelchair user you should be able to travel by bus if there is a wheelchair space available and the bus is not full. But you may find you can't if:

- o your chair is very heavy or very big - taking up a space when you are in it of more than 700 mm wide or 1200 mm long
- o you need to travel with your legs fully extended or the backrest reclined.

You must make sure that your wheelchair is in a safe condition to travel. If you have a powered chair you must make sure that the battery is secure. If your chair has adjustable kerb climbers you should check that they are set so that they don't catch on the ramp.

The bus company has the right to refuse to let you travel if they believe that your wheelchair is not in a safe condition.

Wheelchair priority
Wheelchair users should be given priority over pushchair users. If there is a pushchair in the wheelchair space when you try to board the bus the driver should ask the pushchair user to move. However

if the pushchair user refuses to move, the driver can't force them to do so.

Boarding or alighting

Buses will have different accessibility features, depending on when they were brought into service. Some buses will be fitted with a portable ramp, steps or vehicle lowering systems. If the bus has these facilities, you must be able to use them unless the conditions of the road make it impossible. If you want the driver or conductor to help you get on or off a bus you should ask for assistance. The driver or conductor should help although they can refuse if they have health and safety concerns.

Complaining about the bus service

If you're dissatisfied with disability access to your bus service or the way you were treated by staff you can make a complaint by following the bus company's complaints procedure.

Rights of disabled passengers using trains

Train operators have to make sure that disabled people have reasonable access to rail travel. Under Rail vehicle accessibility regulations disabled people have rights when travelling by train. Disabled people should be able to get on and off trains in safety and without unreasonable difficulty and do so in a wheelchair and travel in safety and reasonable comfort and do so while in a wheelchair.

All trains which came into service after 31 December 1998 must reach certain standards to meet the accessibility needs of disabled people. For example doorways must be wide enough for wheelchairs, there must be a boarding device (a lift or ramp), all floors must be slip-resistant. All trains will have to meet these accessibility standards by 1 January 2020.

Before you travel

You may need assistance when making a journey by train, i.e. help getting on or off the train, ramps for a wheelchair, a visually-impaired person may need to be guided onto the train.

If you need assistance, you should contact the train company that manages the station you're starting your journey from. You can find out which train company you need to speak to and contact telephone numbers for assisted travel through National Rail Enquiries. Most mainline stations have a member of staff who deals with requests for assistance. That person will be able to make any arrangements you need with other trains companies.

If at all possible, you should give at least 24 hours notice before your journey as this allows time for special arrangements to be made. If this is not possible the train companies will usually always still do their best to help, but provide a guarantee to provide their normal level of service.

On the train

On mainline trains there is a space designed for wheelchair users to travel in safety and comfort. You must always use this space and should apply your brakes when the train is moving. If you use a powered wheelchair, you should make sure that the power is switched off when travelling. All intercity train services and most other mainline services are wheelchair accessible. Access to the train is provided by a ramp kept either at the station or on the train.

Wheelchair accessible sleeper cabins are available on overnight trains between London and Scotland but not on those between London and the West of England.

Most local and regional train trains can accommodate wheelchair users. New trains also have facilities to assist sensory impaired people - for example, public information systems that are both visual and audible. An increasing number of trains have wheelchair accessible toilets. You can find out about the facilities on any train when booking your ticket.

It is important to note that train staff have a legal duty to make reasonable adjustments to accommodate disabled passengers, for example, allowing you to travel in first class on a standard class ticket if the accessible toilet in standard class is out of order.

Some train companies have trains that cannot accommodate mobility scooters. Contact the train company before travelling to check they can safely accommodate your scooter.

Complaining about a train company

If you're dissatisfied with disability access on your train service or the way you were treated by staff you can make a complaint. You should try and check the station or train operator's disabled people's protection policy. This will be available from the company's customer services officer or on their website. If the train company hasn't followed the policy, you can complain, using the train company's complaints procedure.

Find out contact telephone numbers for assisted travel through National Rail Enquiries Tel – 0845 748 4950. If you aren't happy with the way a train company deals with your complaint you can appeal, outside London, to: Passenger Focus (tel: 0300 123 2350).

In London-London Travel Watch at:
http://www.londontravelwatch.org.uk/ (tel: 020 3176 2999).

Disabled people and air travel

As with other modes of transport, UK airports are covered by the rules in the Equality Act 2010. They must provide facilities and information that can be used by everyone whatever your needs. For example, if you're in a wheelchair or you're visually impaired, you should be able to read departure boards easily or be able to access all areas of the airport.

Reserving seats

If you book your tickets on-line, there should be sections on the on-line form you can fill in to give the airline notice of the help you are likely to need. If you book your tickets over the phone, or face-to-face, you should be given as much information as possible to make sure you can make a booking that's suitable for your needs.

Get any confirmation that you need assistance in writing. This means you will have proof that you made a special request if the help you need isn't available when you fly and you need to take this further. You should be allowed to book seats which meet your particular needs. If the airline doesn't pre-book seats you should be allowed to board the plane before other passengers.

At the airport

You should contact customer services at the airport if you need help to move through the airport from check-in, through security to the departure gate. For staff to help you, you must give at least 48 hours notice before you are due to fly, turn up at the agreed time, and give yourself enough time to move through the airport. As with all passengers, it is recommended that you turn up at least two hours before departure. If your flight is changed, the airport should still make reasonable efforts to try and help you.

However, the airline should also tell you that it may not be possible to guarantee your seat if there is problem. For example, it may be that someone with a greater need than you needs the seat, or there's a change of plane with different seating arrangements. If your seat does have to be changed, staff should still make every effort to find a way to accommodate you.

The airline will usually have its own policy about how it can help you if you need extra seats because of your disability and the number of bookings it will accept may be limited, depending on when and where you fly.

Moving around the airport

The airport has a legal duty to help you with the following things when you arrive:

- o make sure airport staff know you have arrived and if necessary meet you at an agreed meeting point. This could be either inside or outside the terminal
- o help you move from the meeting point to check-in
- o help you check in your baggage
- o help you get from check-in to the plane, taking you through passport control, customs and security checks
- o board the plane with assisted help if you need it
- o settle into your seat
- o help with your cabin baggage
- o help to get from your seat to the aircraft door
- o help you get off the aircraft, with assisted help if you need it
- o help you get to baggage reclaim and go through passport control, customs and security
- o help you get to a point where you can carry on with your journey
- o help with connecting flights
- o help you to reach a toilet.

Complaining

If you have a problem with the help you've got from an airline or airport because of your disability or reduced mobility you may want to complain. It is recommended that you should first do this directly with them and try and sort out the problem. If you can't manage to sort out the problem, you can complain to the Civil Aviation Authority (CAA) at the address below:

Gatwick Airport South
West Sussex RH6 0YR
Main Switchboard: 0330 022 1500

Rights on the plane

You should always let your airline know of any special needs at least 48 hours before you fly. However even if you don't give 48 hours notice, the airline should still make reasonable efforts to help you.

An airline can't refuse to let you to board the plane because you're disabled or have reduced mobility. However, they can refuse to let you to fly if:

- o you haven't told your booking agent, tour operator or airline that you have a disability or reduced mobility at least 48 hours before you fly
- o there are safety reasons which prevent you from flying - for example you're flying alone but you need help to get about safely
- o the aircraft doors are too small.

If there's a safety reason that you can't fly or the aircraft doors are too small, the airline should try to find another way of getting to you to your destination. If this isn't possible, you should be entitled to a refund.

On the plane

If you're likely to need help to do certain things on the plane, for example fastening your seatbelt, going to the toilet or getting to an emergency exit, the airline can insist that you travel with someone you know. Airline staff don't have to give you personal care.

Taking equipment on a plane

You should be allowed to take up to two mobility items on board with you that will help you get around. If you need more equipment that needs to be checked in, ask if the airline is willing to carry it.

Disabled people and Taxi travel

Taxi drivers and companies have to make sure that disabled people can get in and out of taxis and minicabs in safety and without unreasonable difficulty. They should also make sure that you can travel in safety and reasonable comfort. It is important to note that licensed taxis are only required to be wheelchair accessible in some cities. To find out if there are accessible taxis near you, contact the taxi licensing office at your local council. Another important point is that all taxis and minicabs have a duty to carry assistance dogs.

Ease of use

Their are no national standards for wheelchair accessible taxis and minicabs. Local authorities are in charge of accessibility policies. In London all taxis must be able to carry a standard wheelchair. To find out more about the situation in your area you should contact your local authority.

All drivers must make reasonable adjustments by changing practices, policies and procedures which put disabled people at a serious disadvantage when trying to use their services. Making reasonable adjustments includes: the driver guiding or helping you into the vehicle; helping you to get out of the vehicle at your destination and the taxi or mincicab firm having a standard training programme to include disability awareness for all drivers.

Drivers of licensed taxis and minicabs must allow you to travel with a guide dog, a hearing dog or any other assistance dog free of charge. A driver can be prosecuted for refusing to let you take an assistance dog or charging extra to carry it. However, a driver may be able to get an exemption certificate. This allows them to refuse to take an assistance dog for medical reasons. If they have an exemption certificate, it must be displayed in the vehicle.

Complaining about taxis and minicabs

You should make your complaint to your local council who deal with taxi licensing. In London, you should complain to the Public

Carriage Office (PCO). You can complain by telephone, letter or email. Website www.pco-licence.co.uk.

To complain about a minicab, also known as private hire vehicles, you should first try and sort out the problem with the minicab firm. If you aren't happy with the outcome or feel your complaint is more serious, you can complain to your local council, most have taxi complaint forms on their websites, in London complain to the PCO.

When you make a complaint about a taxi or minicab, it's helpful to have the vehicle registration number of the taxi or minicab. This will be printed on the number plate or disc, the taxi or minicab licence number, the taxi driver's badge number – which you can normally get from their badge - or the name of the minicab firm.

Disabled people and cruise ships

Cruise ships, as with all modes of transport are affected by the Equality Act 2010. Many cruise ships are now fully accessible to people with a wide range of disabilities providing some of the most exciting, inspiring and best value-for-money holidays that you can find. Newer ships offer purpose built accessible cabins, entertainment venues and facilities, wide gangways and lifts whilst moving round the ship, and accessible embarkation and disembarkation. Many older ships have been adapted to accommodate disabled cruisers, meaning that disability is no longer a prohibitive factor in going on a cruise.

For more information on disabiled access and holidays on cruise ships go to: www.disabledholidays.com

How to claim

Send all of the following to DVLA Swansea:

o   your statement of entitlement (it's at the end of your PIP award letter)
o   the vehicle registration certificate (V5C)

The Blue Badge Scheme
Blue Badge parking concessions-What is the Blue Badge Scheme?
The aim of the Blue Badge scheme is to help disabled people who have severe mobility problems to access goods, services and other facilities by allowing them to park close to their destination. The scheme provides a national range of on-street parking concessions for Blue Badge holders who are travelling either as a driver or passenger.

People who automatically qualify for a badge
You're automatically eligible for a Blue Badge if you:
- are registered as blind
- get the higher rate of the mobility component of Disability Living Allowance (DLA)
- get Personal Independence Payment (PIP) and scored 8 points or more in the 'moving around' area of your assessment - check your decision letter if you're not sure
- get War Pensioners' Mobility Supplement
- received a lump sum payment as part of the Armed Forces Compensation scheme (tariffs 1 to 8), and have been certified as having a permanent and substantial disability

People who may also qualify for a badge
It's worth applying as you might still be able to get a badge. You'll have to fill in an extra part of the application to show why you need one.
You should do this if:
- you have problems walking that are permanent, or that your doctor says are likely to last at least a year
- you can't use your arms
- you're applying on behalf of a child aged over 2 who has problems walking, or a child under 3 who needs to be close to a vehicle because of a health condition

You can find out more about the Blue Badge Scheme and whether you are entitled by contacting your local council. Alternatively, you can contact the National blue badge helpline on 0800 0699 784.

The Motability Scheme
he Motability Scheme helps disabled people get mobile by exchanging their mobility allowance to lease a car, scooter or powered wheelchair. To be eligible to join the Scheme, you need to receive one of the following mobility allowances and must have at least 12 months' award length of your allowance remaining.

Higher Rate Mobility Component of Disability Living Allowance (HRMC DLA)
This allowance is provided by the Department for Work and Pensions (DWP) and can be used to cover the cost of a lease agreement with Motability Operations Ltd. As of 11 April 2018, this allowance is £59.75 per week.As part of its welfare reform programme, the Government has started to replace Disability Living Allowance (DLA) with a new benefit called Personal Independence Payment (PIP) for disabled people aged between 16 and 64. The Motability Scheme works with PIP in the same way as is it does with DLA. For more information, go to dwp.gov.uk/pipOpens in new window . As of 09 April 2018, this allowance is £59.75 per week.

War Pensioners' Mobility Supplement (WPMS)
This allowance is provided by **Veterans UKOpens in new window** and can be used to cover the cost of a lease agreement with Motability Operations Ltd. As of 11 April 2018, this allowance is £66.75 per week.

Armed Forces Independence Payment (AFIP)
A new allowance called Armed Forces Independence Payment (AFIP) was introduced as part of the Welfare Reform Act 2012. Those who receive this allowance will be eligible to join the

Motability Scheme. For more information visit their website. As of 11 April 2018, this allowance is £59.75 per week (this refers to the mobility element, which is the same rate as HRMC DLA and ERMC PIP).

If you are visiting the Car Search or Scooter and Powered Wheelchair Search to compare and choose a Motability vehicle, please refer to the DLA/PIP option when making your allowance choice on the relevant option.

The Attendance Allowance cannot be used to lease a car through the Motability Scheme

You may not have to pay VAT on having a vehicle adapted to suit your condition, or on the lease of a Motability vehicle - this is known as VAT relief.

There are currently over 640,000 people enjoying the benefits of Motability. The following are included in the package:

- A brand new car, powered wheelchair or scooter every three years, or Wheelchair Accessible Vehicle (WAV) every five years
- Insurance, servicing and maintenance
- Full breakdown assistance
- Annual vehicle tax
- Replacement tyres (and batteries for scooters and wheelchairs)
- Windscreen repair or replacement
- 60,000 mileage allowance over three years for cars; 100,000 for WAVs
- Many adaptations at no extra cost
- Two named drivers for your car

The Motability Scheme is directed and overseen by Motability, a national charity that also raises funds and provides financial assistance to customers who would otherwise be unable to afford the mobility solution they need.

Motability Operations is a company responsible for the finance, administration and maintenance of Motability cars, scooters and powered wheelchairs.

To find out more about Motability you should contact them at the address at the end of this chapter.

Use of Public Transport
Travel permits for buses and trains

Most local authorities offer travel permits for children who are disabled and over the age of 5 years. There is normally a charge, as there is with everything and the criteria and availability of the permists will vary according to each authority, generally however, the main criteria is being in receipt of the higher rate of PIP. In some cases, your child's GP may be asked for a supporting letter. Your local council will be able to help in this regard.

Help with taxi fares

Some local councils, but not all, offer help with the cost of Black Cab taxi fares. The criteria is similar to other concessions. You should ask at your local council for details.

Community transport schemes

Many local authorities offer local community transport schemes for people with mobility problems. Again, the local authority will have details of schemes on offer in your area. There is also a national association, the Community Transport Association. The CTA is a national membership association which leads and supports community transport. Address at the end of this chapter.

Wheelchairs

If you have a long-term or permanent difficulty with mobility, getting a wheelchair or scooter, or other mobility equipment, may help you to live more independently.

Again, you will need to consult an occupational therapist who will provide you with the advice appropriate to your specific situation. there are wheelchairs centres in each local authority area and in Scotland and Wales they are called Aritificial limb and appliance centres and in Northern Ireland they are called Prosthetic and Orthotic Aids Centres.

Community and public transport

Your local council may operate dial-a-ride or taxi schemes, for example, using vouchers or tokens. You may also be eligible for a bus pass and/or Disabled Persons Railcard.

****

Chapter 12

Holidays and Breaks for Disabled Children and Their Families

Everyone, whatever their situation, needs a break from their children every now and again. Having a breathing space from caring for a disabled child is no exception. Also, your disabled child is likely to enjoy the opportunity of doing new things with other children and adults and will also probably learn much from the experience.

In addition to breaks away from your child(ren) breaks away with your child are also important and there are many organisations which can help you plan a holiday with your disabled child.

In this chapter we outline some of the possibilities for short-term breaks or respite care, such as family based schemes, play schemes or residential care, and holidays. There is also a list of organisations which may be of use to you.

Respite breaks or short term breaks

Respite care is often used to describe the situation when a child goes away from the family home overnight to give his or her parent/carer a break. In addition, respite care can also apply to care given to a child in his or her own home whilst the parent/carer goes out, and to short-term breaks during the day, such as play schemes.

Many parents find it very hard to be away from their child, even when they really need the break. This is understandable but can be overcome by planning respite care so that you and your child can get to know someone over a space of time before you leave them in charge of your child. Because respite care may be needed in an emergency - if you were taken ill, for example, and there was no one else to care for your child - is it important for you to check out the respite care possibilities at an early stage before any crisis may occur.

Different types of respite care and short-term breaks are listed and described below.

Family Based Respite Care

Family based respite care schemes are usually run by local voluntary agencies or by social services departments. They assess, recruit, train and monitor single people or families who are able to look after a disabled child in their home on a regular basis, like 1 night a fortnight, a weekend per month, or sometimes longer spells like a week or a fortnight on occasions (e.g. once/twice a year) so the parent(s) can go away.

The procedure for recruiting, assessing and approving carers is very thorough and governed by Children Act 1989 guidelines (as amended by ongoing regulations) and is very similar to the procedure for recruiting foster parents. So you can rest assured from the start that the carer matched to your child is as suitable and capable as possible.

The scheme which recruits carers for a disabled child will have information about you and your child, what the child is like, what his or her disabilities are and what his or her likes and dislikes are. They will then match you and your child with a carer they judge to be suitable for your child. They will try and match racial, cultural and religious backgrounds as far as possible. It is then usual for you and your child to meet with the prospective carer and his or her own family on several occasions, at your home and the carer's home, to get to know each other. Only after a few meetings will it be possible for your child to stay overnight at the carer's home.

Family based respite care does not always have to mean overnight care though. Many carers are willing and able to take care of children during the day during the week on occasions (during the school holidays occasionally, for example) or sometimes at the weekend. This can normally be negotiated with the carer and who ever is running the scheme.

Residential Respite Care

Residential respite care units for disabled children are run by health, social services or voluntary agencies. They offer overnight care for your child on an emergency or regular basis, if you meet certain criteria which varies depending on the unit. If you are able to plan your child's first stay, it is always best to visit the unit with your child to meet the staff and look around the facilities. This will mean that parting from your child and seeing your child go away from home will be much easier for you both. You can find out about what residential respite care is available by asking your health professional, social services department or voluntary agency.

Play schemes and After School Clubs

Plays schemes for the school holidays and after school clubs are normally run by the leisure department of your local council, although some are also run by voluntary agencies. They are normally based in schools and offer play activities and outings in a relaxed but supervised environment.

Your child may be able to join the play schemes and clubs run for non-disabled children, depending on what his or her needs are. Special schemes and clubs are also run for disabled children.

Respite Care or Short-term Breaks in Your Home

There may be opportunities for respite care in your home meaning that your child can stay at home whilst you go out. This type of respite care, however, is not normally for overnights. Such breaks will usually be for care during the day, such as 2-4 hours, to give you time to go shopping, see some friends, or simply spend some time alone or with your partner. One of the main national organisations offering this type of care is the Carers Trust, which was a merger between Crossroads Caring For Carers Scheme and the Princess Royal Trust for Carers. They employ carers who go into families once a week for 4 hours or twice a week for 2 hours. Most families receive a maximum of 4 hours per week but this depends on their needs and circumstances. Carers work all hours so it is possible to have help at weekends and evenings as well as during the day. Carers Trust carers work with children and people of all ages and all disabilities.

Some local Crossroads Caring for Carers schemes also offer an occasional night sitting service if your sleep is often interrupted.

Some areas may not have a Carers Trust scheme but will have a similar scheme which works under a different name. Ask the Carers Trust national organisation (address at the end of this chapter) or your local social services department, health professional or voluntary organisation to see if you have a local scheme.

Holidays
Having a disabled child should not mean that you cannot go away. There are many organisations that can help you plan a holiday with your child or who can organise an independent trip for him or her if s/he is old enough.

****

Ch.13

Disability and the Armed Forces

War Disablement Pension
You can claim a War Disablement Pension if you are no longer Serving in HM Armed Forces and you have a disablement (i.e. an injury, illness or disease) that you consider was caused or made worse by service before 6 April 2005. If you think your disablement was caused by service on or after 6 April 2005, you should claim under the Armed Forces Compensation Scheme. Claims can be made for both physical and mental conditions.

There are no time limits for claiming under the War Pension Scheme but claims can only be considered once your service has ended and payment will usually be made from the date of claim

Armed Forces Compensation Scheme (AFCS)
AFCS provides compensation for any injury, illness or death which is caused by service on or after 6 April 2005. The War Pension Scheme (WPS) compensates for any injury, illness or death which occurs up to this date. The AFCS is a no-fault Scheme which means payment is made without admitting fault. It is entirely separate from any other personal accident cover, such as PAX or SLI. Therefore, any accident cover that you may already hold is not taken into account when determining an AFCS award.

All current and former members of the UK Armed Forces, including Reservists, may submit a claim for compensation. Unlike the War Pension Scheme, you can submit an AFCS claim while still serving, as well as after you have left the Armed Forces. While there are time limits, above all you should submit a claim for compensation at a time which is best for you. In the event of service-related death, the Scheme pays benefits to eligible partners and children. An 'eligible partner' is someone with whom you are cohabiting in an exclusive and substantial relationship, with financial and wider dependence.

The Service Personnel and Veterans Agency (SPVA)

On 1 Apr 2014, the Service Personnel and Veterans Agency (SPVA) merged with Defence Business Services, thereby creating one of the largest shared service centres in Europe, providing support for all armed forces and civilian personnel as well as providing veterans support . There is no change to any of the services they provide to our customers.

For more information about services to veterans visit their website www.veterans-uk.info or ring our Veterans UK helpline on 0808 1914 2 18.

You can also contact them by email veterans-uk@mod.uk

Veterans UK

www.veterans-uk.info

As detailed above, Veterans-UK is the name used for the veterans advice services provided by Defence Business Services. It's the first stop for veterans who need help and support. A veteran is anyone who has served in HM Armed Forces, regular or reserve including National Servicemen. Veteran's status also applies to former Polish forces under British command in WWII and Merchant Mariners who have seen duty in military operations. Veterans can be any age from 18 to 100 plus. Veterans need not have served overseas or in conflict.

Veterans Welfare Service

The Veterans Welfare Service (VWS) is committed to enhancing the quality of life for Veterans and beneficiaries of pensions and compensation schemes, and all their dependants. It also focuses upon providing support that will enable the seamless transition from Service to Civilian life, assist bereaved families or respond to key life events that present welfare needs. It achieves this by adopting a single central coordinating role that facilitates access to all appropriate services.

The VWS provides a caseworker approach that offers professional help and guidance through either telephone contact or a dedicated visiting service, Under Veterans UK the VWS works in collaborative partnerships with the tri-Services, ex-Service charities, statutory and non-statutory bodies, local community service providers and Veterans Advisory & Pensions Committee's to deliver a quality welfare service that promotes independence, maintains dignity and provides continuous support through life.

The Veterans Welfare Service has four Welfare Centres, providing advice and support across the UK.

The contact details for each office are:

Norcross (based near Blackpool)
Tel 01253 333494
Email SPVA-VWSNorcross@mod.uk

Kidderminster (based in Worcester)
Tel 01562 825527
Email SPVA-VWSKidderminster@mod.uk

Centurion (based in Gosport)
Tel 02392 702232
Email SPVAVWSCENTURION@SPVA.mod.uk

Glasgow (Scotland, NE England, NI and ROI)
Tel 0141 2242709

NHS treatment

If you need an examination or treatment relating to the condition for which you receive a war pension, you are entitled to be given priority for NHS services, subject only to the needs of emergency and other urgent cases.

If you experience difficulty arranging treatment, tell the War Pensions treatment Section. In certain circumstances, your doctor may be able to arrange for you to be admitted to a Ministry of Defence services hospital for the treatment of the disability for which you receive your war pension. If so, you will be eligible for help with travelling costs.

Equipment for mobility

If you need equipment as a result of the disability for which you receive a war pension, you will be able to get advice from the The Veterans Welfare Service . Equipment such as wheelchairs, artificial limbs, or home nursing equipment can be obtained from the NHS. The organisations and charities below may also be able to assist in providing or funding equipment for your special needs.

The Royal British Legion is the nation's leading Armed Forces charity providing care and support to all members of the Armed Forces past and present and their families. They can provide advice on disability claims, loans for home improvements, run residential care homes, offer holiday breaks for carers and much more. Tel: 0808 802 8080 Website:. www.britishlegion.org.uk

BLESMA (British Limbless Ex-Servicemen's Association) assists men and women who have lost their limbs through service in the armed forces or as a result of it. BLESMA provides permanent residential accommodation, gives advice on pensions and allowances, provides financial assistance to members and widows, runs a welfare visiting service, plans and organises rehabilitation programmes for amputees an helps in finding suitable employment. Tel: 0208 590 1124 Website: http://www.blesma.org

The **Burma Star Association** provides a welfare service and gives free and confidential advice to all holders of the Burma Star. Tel: 0207 823 4273.

Website:http://www.burmastar.org.uk

Combat Stress is the UK's leading military charity specialising in the care of Veterans' mental health. They look after men and women who are suffering from a psychological condition related to their Service career. This might be depression, anxiety, a phobia or PTSD (Post Traumatic Stress Disorder). Their services are free of charge to the Veteran.

Website: www.combatstress.org.uk

The "Not Forgotten" Association provides holidays, television sets, licences, outings, excursions and entertainment for disabled ex-service people. Tel: 020 7730 2400

Website:http://www.nfassociation.org/

The Royal Air Forces Association gives advice and financial assistance to serving or ex-serving RAF personnel and their dependents through a network of branches. Each branch has an honorary welfare officer who will assess requests for help and complete the appropriate forms for assistance. The Association also runs a nursing home and three convalescent home together with supportive and sheltered housing schemes.

Tel: 0800 018 2361 Website: http://www.rafa.org.uk

The Royal Alfred Seafarer's Society provides accommodation for ex-members of the Royal Navy and Merchant Navy at three separate establishments in Surrey and Sussex, offering, respectively, sheltered housing, residential and nursing care.

Tel: 01737 353763 Website:

http://www.royalalfredseafarers.co.uk/

SSAFA Forces Help offers welfare help, advice and support to serving and ex-serving members of the armed forces, including partners, widows/widowers and dependent children. They also help obtain equipment and aids and provide specially designed permanent and holiday accommodation for disabled people, and residential care homes. Local branches nationwide and in Eire can raise grant aid through service charities and other sources. Contact local Branch (see local phone book) or the Welfare Department at Central Office.

Tel: 0800 731 4880. Website:http://www.ssafa.org.uk

****

Chapter 14

Useful Contacts

The Law and Disability

Disability Law Service
The Foundry
17 Oval Way
London
SE11 5RR
www.advice.dis.org.yk
advice@dis.org.yk
Free legal advice 0207 7919 800

Gov.uk
www.gov.uk/rights-disabled-person

The Benefit System

Attendance Allowance helpline 0845 605 6055 or 0345 605 6055
(textphone: 0845 604 5312)

Carer's Allowance Unit 0800 731 0122 (textphone: 0800 731 0317)

DWP Bereavement Service:

Bereavement Service helpline Telephone: 0800 731 0469 Welsh
language: 0800 731 0453 Textphone: 0800 731 0464 Welsh
language Textphone: 0800 731 045

Department for Work and Pensions (DWP) on 0800 731 7898 (textphone 0800 731 7399).

Disability benefits Advice
www.gov.uk/disability-benefits-helpline

Jobcentre Plus https://www.gov.uk/contact-jobcentre-plus

Pension Credit claim line 0800 99 1234 textphone: 0800 169 0133

Royal National Institute for the Blind 0303 123 9999 www.rnib.org.uk.

Tax Credit helpline 0345 300 3900 (textphone 0345 300 3909).

TV Licence concessions 0300 790 6071

Universal Credit helpline 0800 328 5644 (textphone 0800 328 1344).

Victim Support line 0808 1689 111 www.victimsupport.org.uk

Winter Fuel Payments Helpline 0845 915 1515

Carers and Help For Carers

Carers Trust
Tel: 0300 772 9600
www.carers.org

Help and Advice on caring-Carers UK
20 Great Dover Street, London SE1 4LX

t: 020 7378 4999

Carers Wales

Unit 5
Ynys Bridge Court
Cardiff CF15 9SS t: 029 2081 1370

Carers Scotland

The Cottage
21 Pearce Street
Glasgow G51 3UT **t:** 0141 445 3070

Carers Northern Ireland

58 Howard Street
Belfast BT1 6JP t: 02890 439 843

Helping hands Home Care Specialists
www.helpinghandshomecare.co.uk
0333 122 4087

Carers Direct NHS Choices
www.nhs.uk/carersdirect

Carers and help for carers Scotland
www.citizensadvice.org.uk**/**carers-help**-and-support**

Wales
ww.carersuk.org/wales

Disabled People and Employment

Access to Work 0800 121 7479 Textphone 0800 121 7579

www.evenbreak.co.uk Jobs for disabled people - Evenbreak matches disabled job seekers with employers looking to build a diverse workforce 0845 658 5717

www.gov.uk/rights-disabled-person/employment

Industrial Injuries-Industrial Injuries Disablement Benefit centre Telephone: 0800 121 8379 0800 121 0314

National Careers Service Helpline 0800 100 900 or Skills Development Scotland 0800 917 8000.

Disabled people and Education

Contact a Family helpline
helpline@cafamily.org.uk
Telephone: 0808 808 3555

Independent Parental Special Education Advice (IPSEA).
https://www.ipsea.org.uk/contact-ipsea

Student finance England www.gov.uk/student-finance

Wales www.studentfinancewales.co.uk

Scotland www.saas.gov.uk

Northern Ireland www.studentfinanceni.co.uk

Care Homes

Care Homes-Support and Guidance NHS Choices
www.nhs.uk/conditions/social-**care**-and-support-guide/**care**

Whilst You Are in Hospital

Disabled People Rights in Hospital
www.citizensadvice.org.uk/.../nhs-patients-rights

Tenancy Rights and Rights in the Home

Housing Ombudsman
info@housing-ombudsman.org.uk
Telephone: 0300 111 3000

Shelter England
www.shelter.org.uk
Help line 0808 800 4444

Disability Housing Scotland
www.housingoptionsscotland.org.uk

Independent Living For Disabled people
www.scope.org.uk
0808 800 3333
Deals with UK housing advice for disabled

Disabled Children

Child benefit helpline 0300 200 3100:

Council for Disabled Children
www.councilfordisabledchildren.org.uk

Disabled Childrens Partnership
disabledchildrenspartnership.org.uk

Family Fund 01904 550 055 Online www.familyfund.org.uk

Healthy Start Helpline 0345 607 6823 www.healthystart.nhs.uk

www.nurserymilk.co.uk. 0800 612 9448

Help if you have a disabled child
www.gov.uk/help-for-disabled-child

KIDS is a leading disabled children's charity that has been in existence for over 40 years working to enable disabled children and young people and their families www.kids.org.uk

Support for Disabled Children
www.actionforchildren.org.uk

Vaccine Damage Payments Unit Tel: 01772 899 944 www.gov.uk/vaccine-damage-payment.

Disabled People and Travel
Trains
Complaints and information-National Rail Enquiries Tel – 0345 748 4950. If you aren't happy with the way a train company deals with your complaint you can appeal, outside London, to: Transport Focus (tel: 0300 123 2350).

In London-London Travel Watch at:
http://www.londontravelwatch.org.uk/ (tel: 020 3176 2999).

Air Travel
Complaints and information- Civil Aviation Authority (CAA) at the address below:

Passenger Advice and Complaints Team
4th Floor,
CAA House
45-59 Kingsway
London
WC2B 6TE
0300 022 1500

Taxi and Mini cabs
Public Carriage Office (PCO) www.pco-licence.co.uk

Motability
www.motability.co.uk

Blue badge Scheme
www.gov.uk/blue-badge-scheme-information-council

Specialist companies
Access Travel
www.access-travel.co.uk
Te: 07973 114365

Responsible Travel
www.responsibletravel.com Tel: 01273 823 700

Enable Holidays
0871 222 4939

Disability Travel
www.accessiblejourneys.com

*

Disability and the Armed Forces

BLESMA (British Limbless Ex-Servicemen's Association) www.blesma.org

Blind Veterans UK (St Dunstan's since 1915 0800 389 7979 website: www.blindveterans.org.uk/

Burma Star Association Tel: 0207 823 4273.
Website:http://www.burmastar.org.uk

Combat Stress www.combatstress.org.uk

Not Forgotten" Association 020 7730 2400
Website:http://www.nfassociation.org/

Royal Air Forces Association www.rafa.org.uk

Royal Alfred Seafarer's Society
http://www.royalalfredseafarers.co.uk/

Royal British Legion
Tel: 0808 802 8080 Website: http://www.britishlegion.org.uk.

Royal British Legion Scotland
https://www.legionscotland.org.uk

SSAFA Armed Forces Charity Website:http://www.ssafa.org.uk

Veterans UK
www.veterans-uk.info

Offices
Centurion (London, SE and SW England)
Tel 02392 702232
Email: veterans-uk-vws-south@mod.uk

Kidderminster (South and Central Wales, Midlands and East England)
Tel 01562 825527
Email: veterans-uk-vws-wales-mid@mod.uk

Norcross VWC (NW England, Yorkshire and Humber, North Wales and IOM)
Tel 01253 333494
Email: veterans-uk-vws-north@mod.uk

Glasgow (Scotland, NE England, NI and ROI)
Tel 0141 2242709
Email: veterans-uk-vws-scot-ni@mod.uk

If you are supporting a veteran and need further advice, the VWS may be able to help. To locate your nearest centre, call the Veterans UK helpline on 0808 1914 2 18.

Pensions Advice
The Pensions Advisory Service
www.pensionsadvisoryservice.org.uk
Tel: 0800 111 3797

****

Index

**